CHICAGO PUBLIC LIBRARY
SOCIAL SCIENCES AND HISTORY
400 S. STATE ST.   60805

BF
503
.M363
1997

Measuring Up

MEASURING UP

The Performance Ethic in American Culture

James M. Mannon
DePauw University

Westview Press
A Division of HarperCollinsPublishers

All rights reserved. Printed in the United States of America. No part of this publication may be reproduced or transmitted in any form or by any means, electronic or mechanical, including photocopy, recording, or any information storage and retrieval system, without permission in writing from the publisher.

Copyright © 1997 by Westview Press, A Division of HarperCollins Publishers, Inc.

Published in 1997 in the United States of America by Westview Press, 5500 Central Avenue, Boulder, Colorado 80301-2877, and in the United Kingdom by Westview Press, 12 Hid's Copse Road, Cumnor Hill, Oxford OX2 9JJ

Library of Congress Cataloging-in-Publication Data
Mannon, James M., 1942–
    Measuring up : the performance ethic in American culture / James Mannon.
        p.   cm.
    Includes bibliographical references and index.
    ISBN 0-8133-3297-4 (pbk.)
    1. Achievement motivation—Social aspects—United States—History—20th century.   2. Performance—Social aspects—United States—History—20th century.   3. United States—Civilization—1970-   —Psychological aspects.   I. Title.
BF503.M363   1997
303.3´3´0973—dc21
                                                                              97-16789
                                                                                   CIP

The paper used in this publication meets the requirements of the American National Standard for Permanence of Paper for Printed Library Materials Z39.48-1984.

10   9   8   7   6   5   4   3   2   1

R0127214249

CHICAGO PUBLIC LIBRARY
SOCIAL SCIENCES AND HISTORY
400 S. STATE ST.   60605

Contents

4   The Measured Self in the Middle Years   75

**5   Losers, Weepers:
    Dilemmas of the Underclass**   102

Acknowledgments

This book has a long history and many people have helped me at various stages.

Foremost, I acknowledge my debt to Rob Robinson, who not only encouraged me to write this book but was kind enough to read preliminary drafts of some of the chapters. His wise counsel and helpful suggestions are deeply appreciated.

Rudy Seward also read parts of the manuscript and provided insightful comments and material. Rudy, likewise, was a source of encouragement throughout the writing process.

My colleagues at DePauw, Nancy Davis, Tom Hall, and David Newman, were always supportive and at various times helped with ideas and sources. Conversations with Tom Hall on various revisions were especially helpful.

The manuscript was prepared with care and competence by Hope Sutherlin and Tammy Gaffney, my assistants at DePauw. At all times they were cooperative, patient, and cheerful in their work for me. They alone know how much I depended on them.

My family has always been encouraging and inspiring. I would like to thank my stepchildren, Pam, Millie, Beth, and John, and my children, Ray, Sarah, and Susan (herself a budding sociologist). Much of what I have learned about adolescent life in our society I acquired from conversations with my children.

My wife, Sue, deserves special thanks for seeing me through another writing project. I relied on her enormously, as my best friend, for encouragement, counsel, and patience. My appreciation for her many kindnesses is hereby recorded.

Finally, I would like to thank Jill Rothenberg, my editor at Westview Press, for believing in this book and helping it come to life.

James M. Mannon

Measuring Up

1

The Performance Ethic in American Society

This book is about the performance ethic in American culture, about how it operates today in the lives of American adults, adolescents, and children, and about how it results in a particularly modern personality configuration that I call the "measured self." The performance ethic is applied early in our lives, subjecting us all to the constant measurements, evaluations, and appraisals of persons and organizations, and continues virtually to our grave, where others' assessment of our ultimate worth is determined by the expense and expanse of our funeral and burial arrangements. I contend that because of this relentless quest to measure up to the innumerable standards of health, wealth, competence, and so on, Americans are becoming less autonomous, less authentic, and less free.

It is my argument that American adults, adolescents, and children are finding their lives constrained, controlled, and manipulated by pressures toward conformity that are far less visible and direct than those of earlier eras. Because the mechanisms that enforce conformity are less visible and recognizable, Americans are often (but not always) in the uncomfortable and unfortunate circumstances of being controlled or of feeling anxious and constrained without knowing why. My goal is to examine how these recent mechanisms to enforce conformity—the "unconscious" social forces—are operating in American culture and thus affecting the lives of contemporary men and women.

What are the hidden forms of conformity in American culture? I would argue that they are, in part, found in the performance ethic, an ethic that forms the basis of social judgment in much, if not all, of the contemporary United States. Life today means having to measure up to an almost endless variety of performance standards. In all that we do, in all that we are or want to become, we are judged, measured, and constantly evaluated. We must meet socially mandated standards of performance, whether that standard is the age at which we are toilet trained, the level of our family income, or the number of dates we have as a teenager. We are controlled increasingly by the performance ethic and its attendant and myriad pressures to measure up. The self that results can best be described as the **measured self.**

Social Control

The **performance ethic,** that is, our cultural mania for measuring and evaluating people and virtually everything about them, is a form of what sociologists call **social control,** the mechanism that societies use to try to ensure that people adhere to or conform to basic cultural norms and values. One of the ways that social control operates in society is through the process called **internalization.** Internalization occurs as individuals "incorporate within their personalities the standards of behavior prevalent within the larger society."[1] Often these standards become so familiar to us that we no longer question their legitimacy. They develop a "taken-for-granted" reality; the standards are almost part of our nature.

As this internalization applies to the performance ethic, it becomes incorporated into our personality, and therefore it doesn't have to be imposed or mandated. No one is shot or fined for refusing to measure up or for refusing to subject him- or herself to unremitting evaluation. Informal means of social control, such as gossip, teasing, or ridicule, keep people in line and ensure that people will do their best to meet expectations and perform well. We feel bad about ourselves if we don't measure up, and we feel good when we perform successfully, whether measured by grades, promotions, popularity contests, or some other scale.

Much of this book is about the downside of the performance ethic. For although some adults, adolescents, and children enjoy the rewards of successful performance and derive much satisfaction in their pursuit of the measured self, many neither find personal satisfaction in such pursuits nor achieve societal approval and reward. Many pay dearly when they fail to measure up, or they attempt to drop out of the performance culture altogether. And we cannot be blind to the human suffering produced by the worst excesses of the performance ethic, for surely there is a linkage between our cultural mania for evaluation and measured performance and our troubling suicide rate, for our drug-abuse problem, and for the prevalence of eating disorders among women and of alcoholism among men and women across several age groups. Performance anxiety, the fear of failing to measure up, has permeated our education, our home lives, our work, and even our leisure. And I believe a form of performance anxiety is connected to some of the more regrettable and publicized self-destructive behaviors exhibited by people in our society.

My focus in this book is confined to those segments of American life that seem most vulnerable to the performance ethic. Thus, I am taking a quasi-developmental approach, examining the performance ethic through what sociologists call the life cycle, from the earliest years of childhood and family life through adolescence and ultimately through the period of what we Americans now call midlife. The developmental analysis is augmented by brief excursions into the performance ethic in the world of sexuality and in the workplace. The book continues with a look at poverty and unemployment in our society and shows how measurement mania in the economy is producing a permanent class of people, mainly minorities, who have little chance now of "making it" economically in the United States.

The Social Roots of the Performance Ethic

Sociologists try to discover the social and cultural factors in human action and behavior. If it is accurate to say that many Americans are trapped in a performance culture and are constantly trying to measure up to objective standards of evaluation and performance, we still need to ask where these pressures come from. If part of the answer is that the performance ethic is rooted in American culture, we still need to ask how that ethic or value came to be. What is or was the social "soil" that allowed the performance ethic to be planted and grow?

We begin our search by looking at a central idea developed by the late-nineteenth-century German sociologist Max Weber, who undertook to explain the social transformations that gradually changed European society from a rural, feudal, religiously dominated society to an industrial, urban, secular, technologically run society. The transforming variable in all this for Weber was the growing rationalization of Western societies. Weber felt that the centuries-old bases for social order—tradition, religion or mystery, habits, and sentiments—were being replaced gradually by an increased emphasis on **rationality,** that is, by an emphasis on objective logic, demonstrable fact, and reason as the bases for action.

This growing rationality, which began to take hold in the fifteenth and sixteenth centuries, was subtly reshaping European society and producing the new cultural values of efficiency, objectivity, calculability, and control. Let's look at each of these values briefly because they are important for an understanding of the performance ethic.

Efficiency requires searching for the most cost-effective (least expensive, fastest) means for producing a result. As populations increase, cost-effective means for organizing, producing, and administrating are favored.

Objectivity calls for people to be morally and emotionally neutral in their actions and evaluations. Rational thinking is valued over sentiments and emotional considerations.

Calculability, the susceptibility to quantification of human action, effort, and ability, is most highly valued. Numerically rating, assessing, and comparing people is thought to be a more precise and reasonable way to judge people than merely subjectively or intuitively judging them.

Control emphasizes plans, forecasts, performance appraisals, and so on to ensure that little of human action is left to chance or accident. Human actions should be controlled, predicted, documented, and assessed to make social order more stable.

Grading students, for example, involves each of these values. Millions of students must be evaluated in school each semester to determine who should pass. Letter grades are efficient (fast and inexpensive); they are considered objective (the teacher is emotionally neutral); they can be calculated in terms of averages (grade point averages—GPAs); and they effectively control students' behavior (students study hard to get high grades).

Weber's argument, then, is that as each of these values (efficiency, objectivity, calculability, and control) becomes increasingly enmeshed in the structure and culture of Western society, a gradual bureaucratization of social life results. Whether at work, at school, in church, or even at play, people's lives are gradually more highly organized and structured around bureaucratic principles and values. Hardly anything is left to chance. Let me cite a modern example: Whereas once boys had fun by getting together to play baseball in the streets by themselves, with improvised rules and equipment and no sense of schedule, today boys "learn" to play baseball by being coached by adults in Little League teams that are highly structured as to rules, schedules, tournaments, uniforms, equipment, and all-star consideration. Whereas once boys played to fill free time, they are now drafted into highly organized teams in league competition. (The analogy also applies to other team sports, such as soccer, basketball, or football.)

To return to my argument, early on the values of objectivity, calculability, efficiency, and control were of importance mostly to economic activity and were thus instrumental in shaping the industry-capital economic system. However, and as Weber suggested, eventually these values spread to all other social institutions, to all other human activity and social patterns. Thus, religious life, schooling, science, art, music, and even popular pastimes such as "eating out" have become imbued with these values: As George Ritzer has discovered, fast-food restaurants are now "rationalized" establishments leaving little to chance or personal custom.[2]

Sociologists maintain that once a value becomes embedded in a culture (whether through culture change, borrowing, or diffusion), it lives on as a "taken for granted" reality. That is, the value becomes accepted by most persons in the culture as an absolute, as an unquestioned truth, or as part of the eternal nature of things. The performance ethic, then, rooted in the values of control, efficiency, calculability, and objectivity, has come to be experienced as an absolute. Eventually we want to be evaluated, appraised, and judged because it is that sense of our self that is most comfortable in this culture. Look at the lives of young people in our society: The fact that children lead highly structured lives, tightly organized around school activities, sports, and structured leisure, is hardly questioned by parents. Children themselves seem to accept the structured routines put upon them. It no longer seems odd to college students that to keep track of their busy schedules they tote with them their appointment books, in which they pencil in meetings with professors, exam dates, jogging times, and so forth. I'm reminded of an old cartoon in which a busy corporate executive is asking his secretary to "pencil in" for him thirty minutes for prayer.

The rationality of social life not only forms the basis of organized, bureaucratic life, but it also stimulates the emergence of three other important twentieth-century phenomena: consumerism, scientism, and professionalism. In a sense, the cultural performance ethic undergirds consumerism, scientism, and professionalism.

Consumerism values having things that can be bought in economic markets. What one can buy often defines one's selfhood in American society. Sociologists maintain that the self is a social product, that is, that we become "selves" as we participate in society and interact with others. Consumerism encourages a concept of a self defined in terms of having things. You are what you have or can buy. Or to put it as Karl Marx did over a hundred years ago, in a consumer society "having replaces being." Rationality permeates consumerism in that shopping, purchasing, and owning depend on the worth of goods, advertising is thought to be objective truth, and economics tell people how to make efficient use of their money. All of us in modern society are raised to be wise and serious shoppers and are taught, albeit in subtle ways, that personal desires, such as for power, attractiveness, success, and even autonomy, can be purchased. We learn that the right product can give us the image or sense of self we desire. Our consumer self, then, has to do with all the ways we try to measure up in the economic marketplace.

Scientism, the value placed on scientific processes and thinking, also has its roots in rationality. Scientists are thought to be persons who reason objectively, who calculate things (mathematically or statistically), and who try to predict the outcome of events based on these objective calculations. This is true not only of the physical and natural sciences, such as biology or chemistry, but also of human and social sciences. For example, psychology purports to be an objective and calculable study of human behavior. Psychologists are thought to be able to predict (at least to some extent) how certain people will behave on the basis of measurements of such human traits as intelligence or drives or motives.

One of the modern effects of scientism is the idea that there are objective criteria of human and social performance. The measurement of human traits and the transposing of these measurements into scores that can be compared becomes a means by which people can be judged, evaluated, included, excluded, or deemed fit or unfit for social goods. Measures of intelligence, scholastic aptitude, and achievement potential infuse not only educational life but other areas of human social life. Work organizations often hire behavioral scientists to evaluate their employees' potentials and psychological assets. Again, the validity of these measurements is a taken for granted reality in our society. Such objective and scientifically derived measures of human ability support the idea of meritocracy in our culture. We want to think that there is an inherent fairness in who gets ahead in our society, in who succeeds and who doesn't. IQ scores, SAT results, achievements scores, and the like are thought to be objective and efficient predictions of who *will* and who *should* succeed and compete best in our society. After all, who can argue with test scores? And what student will have the courage to claim to school authorities or college admission officials that their particular abilities are not really measured well by SAT exams? Low scorers on such aptitude exams are encouraged to keep their performance to themselves.

Finally, **professionalism,** the valuing of expertise, wisdom, and erudition based on years of training and schooling in esoteric knowledge, a value that is closely linked to scientism, is also embedded in the value of rationality. Professionals are thought to be objective, precise, and scientifically infused. Medicine, law, and academics are examples of professions steeped in the tradition of objective knowledge and specialized expertise. Because professionalism is valued in our society, professionals are sought for their advice on matters of which the lay person—that is, the nonprofessional—is thought to be ignorant. Professionals claim expertise in telling persons how to lose weight, gain friends, or become popular. In a society where people are pressured to live up to standards of beauty, body size, achievement, and success, there are professionals in any number of fields, such as sociologists and doctors, to tell people how whatever it is can and should be done. We live in a society dominated by professional expertise and advice, in which lay judgment and knowledge is increasingly devalued.

The Sociological Imagination

Understanding how the American cultural performance ethic controls and shapes people's lives requires that one develop a "sociological imagination." This idea of a sociological imagination originated in the work of C. Wright Mills in the late 1950s, but it remains relevant and insightful today.[3] By **sociological imagination** Mills meant the ability to connect one's personal troubles with the public issues of the day. Personal troubles, Mills argued, are the private, immediate troubles that everyone faces at some point in his or her life. Personal crises may include flunking out of school, failing to obtain a job in the field one is trained for, or lacking sufficient income to supply one's family with basic necessities. Public issues, on the other hand, have to do with contradictions and crises in institutions or large-scale social arrangements. The economy begins to collapse or divorce rates soar or political terrorism abounds. Mills believed that many people feel trapped in their lives because they fail to connect their personal troubles with the major public issues or institutional crises of the day. Instead, they seek to understand and solve their personal troubles only within the most immediate environment and contexts of their lives. By failing to connect their personal troubles with the contradictions and major issues of the day, they fail in the kind of sociological imagination that can "untrap" their lives. Consider the following examples of failure to tap a sociological imagination.

A single parent's third-grade daughter consistently brings home from school poor grades and teacher warnings about other scholastic deficiencies. The single parent may blame herself for poor parenting skills and lack of proper supervision, fret about having passed on genes for lower intelligence, or berate her daughter for not trying hard enough. For both the parent and the third-grader, getting poor grades is a private trouble, a failure to measure up as a parent and as a student. The key public issues here, however, involve the institutions of both education and the economy. Perhaps economic realities necessitate that the single parent work full-time, so that she has little time to spend with her child. Most single parents in our society must work to make ends meet, as child support payments are rarely sufficient and often are not forthcoming in the first place.

Or consider modern schooling. Grades are a cost-effective means of evaluating large numbers of students in educational bureaucracies. Grades are thought to be objective measures of a student's knowledge and scholastic achievement. Students with "high" grades are thought to be doing better than those with "low" grades. The third-grade girl is considered deficient because of her low grades. But there is an institutional contradiction here in using grades as a measure of student performance. What evidence is there that grades always measure what a student has learned? Some students with high grades may have learned very little, and some students with low grades may have learned a lot. Nor are grades always an indication of how hard a student is working. Whatever the case, the sociological imagination requires this single parent to connect her troubles as a working mother of a child with poor grades to the economic and educational conditions of the era in which she is living.

Eating disorders among college women is another example. Each college woman with an eating disorder tends to see her "disorder" or problem within the context of her immediate life at college. That is, she focuses on the way her disorder is compromising her ability to stay in school, on the possible embarrassment she is causing for her friends, or on concern for her own health. But what are the public issues here? First, there are thousands of women students today on college campuses throughout the country who are experiencing eating disorders. Eating disorders are not limited to a few, isolated college women or to a few colleges; the public that is affected here is quite large. Campus therapists and counselors are now recognizing that eating disorders among college women are among the more frequent problems they confront in their work. Second, eating disorders are related to our cultural obsession with thinness, especially for women. The cult of thinness is part of the performance ethic in our society, and it involves another basic contradiction of modern life. Modern high-yield agriculture and efficient transportation systems make it possible, at least, for everyone in our society to eat well, and our lifestyles encourage us to indulge in high-calorie snacks and fast foods. At the same time, technology has also reduced the need for people to expend lots of calories in day-to-day living: Machines do a lot of the hard drudgery work whereby people used to burn off the calories they took in. Thus, our cultural value of thinness is in contradiction to the economic and technological realities of our lives. It is very difficult for most Americans to remain thin today. The pressure on women to remain thin is enormous, though, and is a sure stimulus to eating disorders among college women.

The sociological imagination requires the individual college woman with an eating disorder to connect her private trouble to the public issues of the thousands of women with eating disorders and the cultural values that extol thinness.

The Performance Ethic as a Public Issue

The sociological imagination, the ability to connect private troubles with public issues, sensitizes us to the performance ethic as a public issue. The pursuit of the measured self is often antithetical to other cherished cultural values, such as human freedom and autonomy. We often feel caught or trapped in this contradiction.

One of our core cultural values (expressed, for example, in the writings of American authors such as Ralph Waldo Emerson, Nathaniel Hawthorne, and Henry David Thoreau) is the idea of human freedom, of an individual's right to (in Thoreau's words) "keep pace with . . . a different drummer," to heed the inner voice of conscience in matters of individual decisions. Thus, a **cultural contradiction** is created—a societal tension between two cultural values that may be *incompatible*. The performance ethic, on the one hand, requires conformity to measures and standards determined by anonymous and remote others in institutional authority.

Standardized tests, merit pay systems, thinness norms, management by objectives, and so on are forms of social control to guide individual behavior toward conformity. On the other hand, the value of individualism or personal autonomy encourages a more inner- and self-directed orientation to satisfy personal desires and yearnings.

These cultural contradictions lead to ambivalences in the selfhood of many Americans. One part of a person's self-identity is the result of his or her unique and personal agendas, feelings, and desires, while other parts are expressed in the "measured self," that is, in the self that results from the desire to live up to and conform to anonymous standards of looks, success, and achievement. I contend that most Americans expend a good deal of energy trying resolve these ambiguities in their identities and that that resolution is not easily accomplished. Nowhere, and with no more comical results, is this ambivalence expressed than in the daily escapades of the cartoon character "Cathy" who graces the pages of most U.S. newspapers. In a recurring theme, episode after episode, Cathy is shown trying to cram her chubby little body into a miniskirt or bikini suitable for supermodels. As her frustration and disappointment mount, she comes to realize that her figure will never "measure up." Now angry, hostile, and bitter, she screams that men will just have to love her for her attractive personality!

Herein lies the dilemma for many in this society: Often our individual sense of self-worth and esteem is threatened or negated by what our "measured" self desires or fails to accomplish. For example, innately a student may feel that he or she is smart, may enjoy learning and work hard in school, and may be satisfied in that regard. But when the SAT results come back with a score of 950 and friends are averaging over 1100, the student starts to doubt his or her self-worth and competence. And our culture doesn't help much. On the one hand, we are told and we have learned that personal feelings are worthwhile and important and that if people do their best then the results don't matter. On the other hand, in the performance culture, how one scores in relation to others is as important as how one feels about one's effort, and realistically a low SAT score just might close certain doors of opportunity. One's GPA, another objective measure of potential and achievement, had better make up for a low SAT score if one is to have a chance to reopen those doors. Regardless of how we might feel about ourselves, these feelings are always subject to doubt when our "measured" self leads into fields of competition and performance where our ratings, scores, and standards reflect back on the kind of person we and *others* think we are.

As you read the chapters that follow in this book, develop your own sociological imagination by transcending your personal troubles in measuring up (as a student, parent, friend) with the public issues and cultural contradictions involved.

Key Terms

1. Measured Self
2. Performance Ethic
3. Social Control
4. Internalization
5. Rationality
6. Efficiency
7. Objectivity
8. Calculability
9. Control
10. Consumerism
11. Scientism
12. Professionalism
13. Sociological Imagination
14. Cultural Contradictions

Review Questions

1. What social forces in our society result in the measured self?
2. What are some of the negative results of the performance ethic?
3. Trace the social roots of the performance ethic.
4. What roles do consumerism, scientism, and professionalism play in undergirding the performance ethic?
5. What is the sociological imagination? Why is it important?
6. What do we mean when we say that societal norms and values are "internalized"?

Discussion Questions

1. In your life, which measurements of your selfhood are least comfortable for you? Which measurements are most comfortable?

2. How do you think of yourself when you are unsuccessful at something? How do you cope with disappointment in your strivings?

3. Do you feel our society is overly structured and too highly organized? Why or why not?

4. How do you handle performance anxiety? Do you feel your methods are always successful and healthy?

5. Why do you think it is that most people do not or cannot connect their private trouble with public issues? Are today's public issues more complex than those of the past?

2

Measuring Up
in the Early Years

As we learned in Chapter 1, society and culture anchor themselves in us; that is, cultural norms (definitions of right and wrong) and cultural values (conceptions of the desirable) work their way into our identities and become part of our sense of self, of our sense of who we are.

This process of identity formation occurs throughout our lives as we constantly internalize our cultural norms and values, but in the early years of life a more formal socialization process takes place. By **socialization** sociologists mean the process whereby we learn to be and to do what is expected of us. And in our earliest years, as toddlers and as children, we learn about society through two basic institutions: the family and the school. Social **institutions** are networks of relationships (such as parent-child or teacher-student) that are embedded in shared understandings (common values, norms, and beliefs); these relationships obligate certain behaviors and expectations. Although the institutions of the family and the educational system are the principal areas of socialization of the young, we cannot overlook the importance of religion and the mass media. The last, in the form of television, videos, and movies, play an increasingly important role in shaping the values and beliefs of young people. However, the media habits of the young are very much influenced by parental authority and the dictates of schooling.

Two approaches are important in understanding the shaping of the identities of young people. Both of these approaches argue that our selfhood is not predetermined but, rather, is derived from our social relatedness. Charles Horton Cooley has suggested that our consciousness of our selves arises from our interaction with others and from what we imagine their judgments of us to be.[1] He called this the **looking-glass self**: We look to others to see a reflection or image of who we are and of and how others regard us. In our earliest years, these others are parents, family members, teachers, and neighbors. Arguing in a similar vein, George Herbert Mead contended that our sense of selfhood is derived in a process of "**taking the role of the other.**"[2] We put our "self" into the other person and see ourselves as an object. Thus, the self is both object and subject. Mead calls these two parts of the self the "I" and the "me." The I is the inner sense of self, the source of the desires and yearnings that we try to satisfy. The me is the social self, the result of the attitudes of the **significant others** (that is, those immediate others in our lives, such as parents or siblings, who have the power to reward us or shame us) in our lives whose judgment we value and whose approval we seek. Often our desires and urges are modified by what we imagine the reactions and judgments of these significant others to be.

*   *   *

Measuring up, then, starts in the home as parents begin to socialize their children into the performance ethic and as children, in turn, develop a self that is accustomed to being evaluated, judged, and assessed. Later, in the schools, teachers reinforce to young people the importance of measured and quantified performance. However, in this process it is not only young people who are being "fitted" for the measured self; parents and teachers are judged, assessed, and evaluated in their roles as well. These persons must live up to the societal standards of good parenting and teaching. Teachers are subject to the bureaucratic evaluations of performance reviews and appraisals. Parents are more informally evaluated by other family members, the community, expert judgments, and so on. Parents and teachers both discover that they are not autonomous, that they are not free to teach and to parent as they feel best. They too must live up to the expectations of others, who stand in judgment of their "performance." It is these issues that I address in this chapter.

In a "Calvin and Hobbes" cartoon, Calvin suggests that all parents be required to sign a liability form accepting legal responsibility for whatever parenting mistakes they make raising their children. Though this Calvin cartoon is meant to be humorous, it also contains a painful truth for young parents in our society today: For many fathers and mothers in U.S. society, where the performance ethic flourishes, raising children to succeed, to achieve, and to measure up has become fraught with untold problems, uncertainties, self-doubts, and ambiguities. "Am I a good mother or father?" "Do I read the right childcare books?" "Am I getting the most up-to-date expert advice?" "Do I listen to the right people about what I should be doing for my kids?" These and similar questions point to the gnawing uncertainties that characterize modern parenting, making it the one contemporary social role that, especially among middle-class professionals, no one enters into lightly.

And why should this be so? Parents have raised children for thousands of years, and in most times and places they did what came naturally or what was dictated by tradition, local custom, or community and village norms. And their children, with some exceptions, grew to adulthood according to the same traditional or community standards. Why is it that parents in our society are so unsure of themselves and their abilities, so fearful and anxious about how their children will turn out, so quick to see their children as having problems, and so ready to seek advice from experts and others whom they believe to be wiser and more knowledgeable than themselves?

The answer to these questions lies in the way the performance ethic, the measuring-up process, has permeated modern U.S. society, making limitless demands on people of all ages and statuses to achieve, to make good, to count for something, and to prove to themselves and to others that they have what it takes to succeed.

Our cultural mandate to succeed and to prove worthy, thus, makes childhood a difficult time for the child and child-rearing a difficult task for parents. And the prevailing wisdom maintains that the earliest years of a child's life are the most crucial in prodding, nudging, and nurturing a child in the tasks and stages necessary to move toward a successful and worthy life as an adolescent and adult. Woe to the parents who fail to recognize their child's achievement "gifts," who are slow to pick up on developmental problems, or who do not provide constant attention and intensive nurturing for their offspring. And pity the poor child who fails to measure up because his or her parents read the wrong books, are blind to his or her shortcomings, are preoccupied with their own needs and desires, or who just don't have what it takes to parent for success.

The measuring-up process actually begins even prior to childhood, as any good obstetrician or obstetric nurse knows. In a culture driven by the performance ethic, not even the newest born, fresh out of the womb, are immune to its influence. One of the very first things that happens to U.S. babies born in a hospital (and most of them are) is that they get measured.

Dr. Virginia Apgar saw to that in 1952 when she developed her now famous and widely accepted **Apgar score,** a numerical scale evaluating a baby's clinical vitality and well-being immediately after birth. Within one to three minutes of the baby's delivery, heart rate, respiratory effort, muscle tone, reflex irritability (measured by thumping the bottom of the baby's foot), and color are each rated on a scale of 0–3 by a nurse trained in Apgar measurement. These individual scores are added up, and a total score in the range of 7–10 indicates a clinically healthy baby; lower scores call for immediate medical intervention, but most babies fall in the upper range of scores.[3] Since American culture in general rewards brainy success more than brawny success (except in professional athletics), obstetricians inform us, and we are pleased to learn, that Apgar scores in the 7–10 range correlate strongly with the absence of neurological distress at age one. Most babies measuring well on their Apgar score are mentally fit at the end of their first year.

The reader should note that I'm not arguing against the use of Apgar measurements. I recognize that the Apgar score serves the primary and very worthwhile purpose of identifying just after birth those babies in physical distress. However, it is more than coincidental that in our culture, which is infused with measurement mania, each baby begins life measured on a 1–10 scale, albeit for his or her own good. Yet I wonder how many new parents might be heard in the corridors of countless maternity wards, mildly boasting to their relatives and friends of how well their baby did on the Apgar: "Yes, she's off to a good start." More to the point, perhaps: How many babies in our society will find their subsequent childhood, adolescence, and adult years filled with numerical measurements of their character, intelligence, competencies, and health, all for their own good? It is difficult to be critical of the use of Apgar scores for newborns, but isn't it also difficult to find fault with the logic and apparent benevolence of IQ tests, personality assessments, popularity ratings, stress-level scores, and myriad other measuring devices that we have developed to evaluate, categorize, and label children, students, and workers in our society? As long as the measurements are objective and scientific and carried out for the person's own good, then they are considered benign.

But I'm getting ahead of myself. Let's return to our newborn baby and the beginning of her innocent measurements. Following the Apgar measurement, nurses diligently record the infant's weight and length and scrutinize her further for any signs of abnormalities. Length and weight proportions are the more familiar and publicly revealed of the baby's measurements, and they serve as the basis of many a parent's bragging in the social world of the maternity ward. What proud father can be restrained from informing relatives, friends, indeed all who will listen and some who won't, about the weight and length of his baby boy? Interestingly, many hospital maternity wards encourage this measurement passion by installing large picture windows in nursery walls through which newborns can be viewed by visitors; some hospitals attach cards to the cribs listing the baby's length and weight. Drawing upon my experiences as a father (two daughters), while peering at my own infants in the nursery, I noticed that the longest and heaviest babies drew the most admiring glances and the most sustained "ooh's" and "aah's" from the gathered visitors.

This is the beginning of the measuring-up process in the United States: the crib, the cradle, the first report card from the attending physician and nurse that the infant is initially OK and that much can be expected. From earliest infancy through toddlerhood, the child's life will become a testing ground, a staging area to assess how well the youngster will do in later life. Though the infant lying innocently and sleepily in the crib cannot know it, even in those earliest few days of the maternity ward all the eyes, professional, paternal, and familial, that look down at the crib, scientifically and lovingly, are also peering judgmentally, looking for signs of future potential. And it will fall upon the infant's parents not only to love but to judge; not only to admire but to assess; not only to accept some traits in their infant but to hunt for and measure many others. And to what end? In American culture, parents' devotion to their newborn is always tempered by their desire to see in the infant something of their own dreams and aspirations, something of their own competences and achievements, something of themselves; in a word, their replica.

We are living in an era in which virtually everyone is expected to grow and develop through various stages and to meet certain standards, and the earliest months and years of a toddler's life are seen as crucial in forming the habits, personality traits, and competences that set the tone for the child's future. The prevailing cultural wisdom in the United States, which for some years now has been heavily influenced by theories of developmental psychology and other scientific and quasi-scientific disciplines emphasizing human development and growth, constantly reminds parents that if children fail in some measurement, corrections should be sought, and the sooner the better. And today's parents can draw from a bottomless well of professional advice, from child psychologists, pediatricians, psychiatrists, social workers, and a host of other "experts on the child." For parents unable to pay the fees associated with private consultation, any bookstore or newsstand has a plethora of magazines, books, handbooks, and manuals on child-rearing, available at reasonable paperback rates.

The Serious Childhood

Are we too obsessed with our children today? And has the performance ethic that drives our culture so relentlessly taken much of the joy and spontaneity out of childhood? Have parents become so concerned with how their children are performing on some measurement scale of development, growth, potential, or achievement-motivation that they are afraid to let their children just "be" and live in the world as children? I think that the answer to these questions is a resounding "yes," that modern childhood is **serious childhood** in which children are grimly prepared for success. Children's lives are less joyous and happy when so much of their activity is under adult, professional, and organizational scrutiny.

Philip Aries, in his scholarly study *Centuries of Childhood*, discovered the truth about our modern obsession with child-rearing.[4] Using historical materials and investigation, Aries found that as recently as the seventeenth century our European ancestors did not have the language to distinguish the stages of childhood. Nor did they have any concept or special age-category for what we know as adolescence. The idea of extended childhood, which is so familiar and taken for granted in our thinking today, did not exist for Europeans prior to the seventeenth century. Artists, for example, merely portrayed children as miniature adults. In other words, Europeans had yet to discover childhood!

Moreover, the age at which children attended school was not standardized; they started and finished pretty much as they or their families pleased. Schools were not divided into age grades; in fact, it was the very concept of age-grade schooling, initiated in the eighteenth and nineteenth centuries, that began to create the notion of childhood itself. Schooling created the possibility of defining childhood as a specific period of life. Aries also pointed out, and this is very important for our understanding of parenting and childhood in American culture today, that in the eighteenth century the family began to separate itself from societal and community influence, and the idea of a private family life gradually emerged. Along with the growth of private family life came a new desire for privacy in personal life and behaviors. Families built houses with separate rooms, such as personal bedrooms or sitting rooms, where individuals could be alone and feel a sense of privacy.

All of this starts to sound very modern (though it occurred only about two hundred years ago) and familiar to us; and who can argue with the need for privacy and a chance to be alone for awhile? But of concern to us here is Aries's contention that as family life became more private, parents grew increasingly concerned with the their children's health, which they tended to connect with their children's progress. Even more important, parents began to see education as necessary for their children; schooling was necessary for their children to progress in a healthy way. Parents got ample support in their ideas from religious moralists who taught that it was the parents' duty to start sending their children to school in early life. Thus, with the firm backing of religious moralists, the family and the school together removed children from adult society. According to Aries, from the eighteenth century on children were no longer *free*; they were constrained and controlled by the authority of the church, the school, and the family. The resulting situation caused Aries to lament: "Our world is obsessed by the physical, moral, and sexual problems of childhood."[5]

Thus, in the space of a few hundred years the idea of childhood took shape, and in many ways this was a remarkable and positive development. Since children were no longer considered miniature adults, they were perceived as having a special age or place in the world, and there is no doubt that there are many positive aspects of an extended childhood. Children are no longer physically mutilated or branded for committing crimes; they are no longer made to work endless hours in unsafe and unhealthy sweatshops; they are no longer apprenticed out to work for other families and treated as servants. We have made noteworthy advances in the quality of life of most of our children today when compared to the lives of children of two hundred years ago.

However, there is another side of the coin that must be faced squarely if we are to create a better world for parents and children. In the process of establishing a special period of life called childhood, we run the risk of becoming obsessed about our children and their growth and progress. Whereas the typical parents in sixteenth-century Europe cared too little about their child's development, we are equally guilty of caring too much. And whereas the child living four hundred years ago had too much freedom and too few expectations, children in our world are not free enough and are under far too much pressure.

There exists a seriousness about childhood in our culture that, if not deadly, is certainly stultifying and constraining for both child and parent. Once the idea of childhood developed in Western societies, it became vulnerable to all the pressure of the performance ethic. Today, not even our children are immune to the performance ethic, as they are pressured to define their selfhood in terms of how well they are performing at school, at play, and on the Little League team or the soccer field; even during their earliest years they are pressured to accomplish their developmental tasks. Let's look at this last activity more closely by returning to an earlier theme.

Soon after parents bring their newborn home from the hospital, they feel the weighty pressure of what is considered to be the monumental task of raising their child properly. Given the infusion of the performance ethic in our culture and urged on by the tenets of developmental psychology, parents are expected to see to it that their child forms all the habits, attitudes, abilities, and personality configurations that will allow him or her to grow and progress to a successful future. Parents are warned that serious mistakes in child-rearing in these earliest months and years might do irreversible damage and mark the child for failure. Today's parent is not so much expected to be a taskmaster as a "child developer," and the sooner parents see themselves as amateur psychologists the better. Any parent who thumbs his or her nose at modern psychology is not fit to be a parent, as any supermarket-shelf parenting magazine can attest.

The curious reader might ask where these ideas about parent-as-psychologist came from, and the answer is provided by author David Elkind, a child psychologist who has written extensively about children and adolescents. In his book *The Hurried Child*, Elkind traces the tremendous increase in interest in child development to a period in the United States shortly after World War II.[6] Interestingly, we learn from Elkind that prior to World War II there were only two professional journals devoted to child development. Within a few decades after the war there were, and still are, more than a dozen. Child development theory and popular psychology found fertile ground in the soil of prosperity that followed World War II, with its expanding middle class and the emergence of the white-collar suburb, and parenting in the United States took a new direction that, with some modifications, remains the same today.

Only a century or two ago, the moral authority over children rested upon the triumvirate of the church, school, and family. Eventually, as societies secularized—that is to say, as the institution of the church diminished as a moral force in controlling and constraining people's attitudes and behaviors—the school and family had to go it alone in shaping the lives of children. However, with the discovery that children can "develop," child-rearing soon became the province of professionals, for (to oversimplify the case) modern psychology has replaced the church in the United

States, partly as a moral force but, even more, as a definer of reality about children, what they are like, and how they should be raised.

David Elkind does not underestimate, and neither should we, the valuable contributions made by child development theory, but he does lament the fact that today's parents want to hurry their children along the developmental path too quickly. Thus, our children now feel pressured to mature and achieve developmental milestones sooner than they are actually able, and they feel compelled to accomplish things they aren't competent to do. If this continues, Elkind argues, we are in danger of losing our sense of childhood.

There is a strong element of truth in what Elkind is saying, but he has not identified *why* parents feel constrained to put so much pressure on their children. And I think the reason is that parents themselves are under enormous pressure to parent for success. Childhood has become overly serious, but so has parenting, and this seriousness is due in considerable part to the performance ethic. Since our expectation is that children become, or "develop," into successful adults, it is absolutely essential in our society that children get off on the right foot, and it is the parents' duty to ensure that their child's progress toward the various rewards of later life is accurately assessed and measured.

The seriousness of childhood begins with the parents' compulsive preoccupation with their toddler's acquisition of such basic human competences as walking, talking, and being toilet trained. The ages at which these abilities are mastered have become cultural mandates, and they are the source of much parental anxiety. A child's inability to acquire these competences at a certain point on the developmental timetable was taken in the 1950s and 1960s as an indication of his or her backwardness, as an indication that the child was a "slow learner." Parents fretted over a child's lack of "progress" because they feared their child wasn't as bright as other children and was hence behind on the track for future success and accomplishment. Fortunately, current child development theory has relaxed and liberalized many of these rigid developmental norms; in fact, today's parents are informed by some groups of experts that each child should develop his or her own timetable, that children must not be pushed too hard—but nevertheless, that they should develop.

Not only is childhood a special period, but it is increasingly a period set off as the time to pick up early warnings of future achievement or potential failure or social stigma. David Elkind contends that childhood is becoming valued less as a stage of life with its own virtue and more as a period in which a youngster's future competences and abilities to measure up are tested and assessed. Parents and other adult authorities are under a cultural mandate to detect and uncover the best in children as well as the worst. Just as each child carries the potential for his or her future achievements and successes, likewise, he or she sows the seeds of his or her own failures, destruction, and stigma. And these potentials and liabilities, the successes and the shortcomings, are, in turn, thought to be nurtured and pruned by parental role models. Correct parenting nurtures success; improper parenting can produce deviants. It is increasingly accepted today that the best in children is the result of good parenting and the worst is the result of parental failure. According to the professional language and ideology of child development, the "early warning signs" of a child's potential achievements and disasters can be recognized, anticipated, and directed either to the promotion of success or the avoidance of disaster; and the parents' role is to accomplish all three.

In our culture, two examples stand out of behaviors that leave parents especially anxious and vulnerable to the charge that they failed their children through their own faulty parenting: juvenile delinquency and homosexuality.

Americans have a love/hate relationship with juvenile delinquency. On the one hand, in movies and on TV we romanticize and idealize the delinquent as a rebel, with or without a cause. Yet we also abhor delinquency and at various times in our history have regarded it as one of our most pressing social problems. Current public thinking connects delinquency to our national decline in economic productivity, to the general cultural malaise, and to other forms of censured behavior, such as drug abuse and sexual promiscuity. In accounting for the pervasiveness of delinquency, both professional judgment and lay opinion place the blame at the doorstep of the home and family; that is to say, the parents of the delinquent are considered the real failures. Since the 1950s, the familiar saying "There is no such thing as a bad child; only bad parents" has become almost axiomatic in our culture as we attempt to affix blame and cause.

Howard James's book *Children in Trouble* is representative of the way in which delinquency was—and to some extent still is—explained and understood for several decades.[7] James devotes an entire chapter to "How Parents Produce Delinquents," as if the process were analogous to the way General Motors produces Camaros. In this chapter, James contends that all of the many teachers, social workers, probation officers, and reform school administrators he talked to agreed that parents, not children, should be the ones sent to jail. And as evidence of where James stands on all this, he goes on to list twenty-two reasons why parents fail their children and produce delinquents. Among the reasons he includes are parental immaturity, parental addiction to TV, and parental failure to build up their child's self-confidence.

Given books such as this, as well as countless equally accusatory magazine articles, television documentaries, and reports by government commissions, is it any wonder that parents pressure their children to hurry through childhood and master developmental tasks? The sooner the child gets beyond the legal age limit of delinquency the better; then, when things go wrong, it is someone else's fault, and Mom and Dad are off the hook.

The other fear characterizing modern parenting is that one's child will fail in proper sex-role socialization and become a homosexual. Perhaps for some parents this is the ultimate fear, given the severity of the social stigma of homosexuality in our culture. Moreover, as Letty Pogrebin points out, the fear remains hidden and unspoken yet is real enough to prevent parents from letting their children be truly free.[8] Pogrebin shows us that parental fear grows out of a specific cultural conditioning that emphasizes that sex roles produce sexuality and that certain "ingredients" create homosexuality in children. For example, if boys are raised to be "real men," to act masculine, brave, and tough, they won't become homosexual. The "ingredients theory" contends that certain of the child's features, such as hormones or early family environment, predispose him or her to homosexuality. Psychoanalytic theory, for example, is one of the "ingredients theories" and holds the family responsible for homosexuality because, as the argument goes, it is the family's duty to teach children proper sex-role behavior so there won't be any mix-ups in sex identity. If a child becomes homosexual it is because the family failed to teach appropriate sex roles, in much the same way that family neglect or parental TV addiction lead to juvenile delinquency.

We can credit Letty Pogrebin for dispelling these dangerous assumptions, as she has amply demonstrated that there is little, if any, scientific evidence linking homosexuality to sex-role socialization or to a specific ingredient. No one knows for sure what causes or produces homosexuality. Yet these fears persist in our society because we fear and have so little tolerance for homosexuality. As long as we feel homosexuality is one of the worst things that can happen to people, neither parent nor child will be free to play their roles as they would like.

Intensive Parenting

In recent years, parenting for success has come to mean constant and **intensive parenting**. The new ideology of parenting decrees that children will acquire attributes and traits necessary for success if parents are constant and intensive supporters, backslappers, morale builders, and role models. What boy will learn to compete today if his dad won't take part in Little League or soccer coaching? And no mom is worthy of the name if she isn't willing to sit for hours behind the wheel of the family's Toyota minivan driving her children from one lesson or day camp to another. The performance ethic in our culture has made it almost mandatory that parents learn to drive, for how else are children going to get to all the lessons so critical to their developmental growth? Children are driven in our society both figuratively and literally. Children are figuratively driven to succeed by the ideology of the performance ethic, as they are literally driven to all their growth-related activities by chauffeur-parents in the family minivan.

The fascinating aspect of intensive parenting is that it comes at a point in our history when divorce has increased the number of single-parent families and economic insecurities have made the two-income family necessary and commonplace. As parents have less time available for their children because of their economic responsibilities, the emerging cultural expectation is that parenting should be intensive, constant, and extremely attentive. Especially among middle-class parents, there is unremitting pressure to keep their children occupied with structured activities and recreation that will bring out the "best" in them. The Organizational Man who was the representative figure in the 1950s has been replaced by the Organizational Child of the 1990s. Permit me to use a personal example to illustrate this.

As a college professor, I reside in a relatively small, quiet Midwestern community where I have had much contact with parents of school-age children. In the past several years, as I have casually observed family life in my community, I've been impressed by the fact that children of middle-class parents rarely appear to have any free time. Even their leisure, recreational, and supposedly "fun" activities are highly organized and overly scheduled, and their parents seem to prefer it this way.

I recall my childhood as being much different. I grew up in the late 1940s and early 1950s in a working-class suburb on Chicago's West Side. Our brick streets and vacant lots were always filled with boys playing ball and girls jumping rope, and there were rarely any adults around. This didn't bother us any. Our parents often reminded us that they were too busy to "watch us play," and we got used to it and enjoyed the freedom that came with being left alone. When we played baseball in the streets, we provided our own equipment, we chose our own sides, and enforced our own rules; in short, our "play" was pretty much up to us. Although we might have missed out on some adult approval by being left to our own devices, we also escaped adult censure and the accompanying disappointment as well. Things have changed.

Today when I inquire about summer plans of my colleagues at the university where I teach, many of them describe schedules revolving around their children's organized activities. Coaching Little League, soccer, tennis, and swimming teams occupy the men, and my female colleagues take their children traveling, to music lessons, ballet lessons, day camps, and so on. Almost every parent I know tries to see that their children take enough lessons to become proficient at something. Perhaps another Monica Seles, Greg Norman, Pelé, or Barry Bonds? No middle-class child in my community can grow to maturity without attending camp, without being part of at least three organized groups, such as 4-H, Boy Scouts, DeMolay, or Brownies, and without spending hours on lessons (to say nothing of the time they spend in the dentist's chair having their braces adjusted). All of these groups and activities depend on parents becoming highly involved as boosters, volunteer coaches, morale builders, and, most important, as uncomplaining chauffeurs. If there is ever another oil embargo, childhood will cease to exist in the United States.

And not many parents that I know refuse to become involved. They want very badly for their children to succeed in life, and they view these activities as terribly instrumental in their child's development for success. For middle-class parents, this is a large part of what it means to do "right" by their children.

I can see emerging among middle-class Americans today a new **Parkinson's Law of Parenting**: Parents (or the single parent) must see to it that organized activity fills a child's every available minute. Parents willingly accept the authority of the schools because they know that the child's day is organized around a balance of task-oriented and expressive activities, and parents feel that this will help their child "grow." And once school is finished, for the day or the summer, parents are quick to structure their child's activities on their own, as they feverishly search for groups and programs that will assist in their child's development. For parents, the implicit function of organized sports, instructional camps, and endless lessons is to promote "growth," and without growth there can be no success.

Barbara Ehrenreich, in her book *The Hearts of Men*, traces the ethic of growth in American culture to the 1960s, when American psychology shifted its view of human nature.[9] Whereas earlier psychologists had defined personal maturity as an accumulation of "growth experiences," according to Ehrenreich during the 1960s psychologists encouraged people to look at life as an adventure and to see that human potential was unlimited. Moreover, people had a responsibility, if they were to tap their potential, to move from one peak experience to another in the search for the actualized self. Individuals were not merely free to grow; rather, they were under a cultural mandate to do so. Psychological growth soon became one of the new measuring rods of the 1960s and 1970s: "How much are you growing in relation to others? How much of your human potential have you tapped? Please give your answer on a scale from 1–10."

It is fairly easy to see how today's parents cling to the notion of growth and want to give their children as many opportunities as possible to unleash their unlimited potential. Whether these parents feel they have tapped all of their own potential, or whether they have had all the self-actualization they want or can stand, they must certainly feel an obligation to give their children the opportunity. And if their children complain or resist, parents need only remind them that signing up for computer camp or tennis lessons is good for them. How else will they discover their potential as systems analysts? How else will they master their ground strokes?

Organized sports, instructional camps, and the endless round of music, dancing, and baton lessons have an underlying seriousness about them that I think many children sense but cannot articulate because they lack the language of protest. Parkinson's Law of Parenting, which drives children into an increasingly organized and structured life, serves to heighten the measuring-up process for children and the pressure they must certainly feel. Whether on the soccer field or at the piano recital, children find that their fun activities are another context in which they are tested, probed, prodded, and expected to "look good" and show potential for even greater future accomplishments. Furthermore, they must accept the rationale that their physical and mental health depend on these activities and that they owe it to themselves and their parents to grow and develop their potentials. As children they must realize that they can never merely content themselves with *being*; they must see their lives as *becoming*, as an unfolding process of growth experiences that never end. The performance ethic for America's children means that today's accomplishments are never ends in themselves; they are only signposts and symbols for potential and growth.

We are robbing children of whatever joy there is in childhood by hurrying them through it and pushing too hard. Our children are under too much pressure to perform and to measure up in the highly structured and organized activities that we, as parents, have devised for them. In some communities, kindergarten and first-grade children are now involved in organized, adult-coached basketball competitions. Every organized child's activity creates an occasion for failure as well as for success, feelings of inadequacy as well as of achievement. Even more insidious and damaging to children than this, however, is that we have allowed much of the psychology of growth and human potential movement as ideologies to color our view of childhood. If children are bundles of potential and if their potentials are unlimited, no childhood accomplishment is of intrinsic value. Nothing a child does can please him- or herself (or parents) except as a sign of potential, as an indication that future accomplishments will be forthcoming, and even these will pale in comparison to the ones that will follow. Such a situation can only heighten the pressures and ambiguities of childhood and parenting alike.

Children are not only vulnerable to the stresses of the performance ethic, since they define their identities in terms of their ability to measure up, but they also develop ambivalent attitudes toward their parents. Children desire, long for, and need their parents' nurturing, love, and intimacy. They seek unconditional and unqualified parental love. Yet in our culture, as they move through childhood, they also seek their parents' approval in performance-related activities. Children want their parents to think they are doing well, whether it is in school, at camp, in recital, or on the Little League field.

To a certain degree, this has always been so; I can remember that as a boy on the streets near Chicago, we always liked it if our parents would take time to watch us play for a while, if we could show off a little. And, of course, a good report card was valued too as a way of seeking approval. Yet that was an era before Little League was fully developed and accepted in suburban culture as an organized arena of competitive pressure; and our fathers were not coaches. (The fathers of the boys in my neighborhood were working double shifts in local factories.) We were advised to do as well as we could in school, not so much because good grades were a sign of our potential (though I had a few teachers who employed such language) but because it was expected that we would do our best. The 1950s, as Ehrenreich and others have noted, was an age of conformity; and decent grades in school were an indication of conformity, of following the rules, and a matter of duty and respect toward parents. In other words, I think there was a greater match between what we as children felt our parents expected of us and what we felt we could deliver.

I'm not sure that this is the case today. For reasons mentioned earlier, good grades and occasional showing off today are valued not as ends but only as growth-enhancing performances and signs of potential for future accomplishments. Children fear that if they don't live up to their potential, they forfeit not only their parents' approval but their love as well. Although I've stated that this problem is generic to all parent-child relationships in the United States, I would like to examine Little League activities as a case in point.

To return to my neighborhood in the 1950s, as boys we played a lot of baseball, but few of us were involved in Little League because the concept was new; it was just beginning to be popular. Our baseball was played on sandlots and in the streets, and adults rarely had anything to do with our games. If my father ever watched me play, it was only briefly; and although I sought to look good when he watched, I was not bothered by my poor play, as we were both accustomed to it. More important, in that era street baseball was mostly *play*; each team tried to win, but it was no shame to lose or to look bad doing so. Besides, if one's team lost there was always the defense that the sides were uneven.

Youth baseball changed from child's play to a serious game with the advent of Little League, when as a sport it was usurped by grown men. In the quiet college community where I now live, it is important not only to win but to look good in the process. The only boys invited to play are those that show potential for high caliber baseball skills. There are major leagues and minor leagues and even a competitive draft system. More significantly, teams are coached by the boys' own fathers. A few of my university colleagues have coached their own sons (while I have assisted), and at times the pressure on the field and in the dugout was ferocious. These coaches were well-intentioned, well-meaning fathers and bright, sensitive, and caring men, but often I saw their sons leave the pitcher's mound with tears in their eyes, when the opposing team was scoring at will. And though the fathers didn't verbalize or overtly convey their disappointment or disapproval, their sons no doubt felt it, as they sensed as well that they were letting their father-as-coach down by pitching so poorly. These were awkward and trying moments for fathers and sons alike, both victims not only of Little League but of the pressure of the performance ethic in American culture.

The father-as-coach phenomenon is the prototype of the parent-child pressures that youngsters experience in their overly organized lives. The child of the 1950s, awkwardly and eagerly showing off at play for his parents, has been replaced by the child of the 1990s, pressured to look good, to perform well, to show potential to father-as-coach or to mother-as-scout-leader. And as parents are increasingly required to assume the more formal roles of supervisor, leader, and director of their children's organized and structured growth activities, the problem of parent–child pressure can only deepen, as the parent/evaluator/judge configuration becomes all the more entrenched and taken for granted. And I am referring here not only to the pressures generated in a highly competitive society but to the more pervasive and less well understood demands placed on people for evaluation and approval. Today children can rarely avoid the evaluative and judgmental context necessitated by the performance ethic. Thus, our children are often torn between their needs for the unqualified love and acceptance of their parents and their conditioned desire to measure up, to grow, and to actualize in ways that will gain their parents' approval.

Stressful Family Ties

David Elkind, in his 1994 analysis of family trends in the United States, argues that family ties have become stressful because of a number of imbalances that exist in family life.[10] Whereas regularity and stability in family life was once assured by a sort of implicit "contract" between parents and children that recognized the obligations of each, today's parents are finding it difficult to uphold their end of the bargain. Middle-class parents are no longer as secure in their income, promotions, and seniority as they once were. Instead, many working parents must constantly upgrade job skills or change occupations to remain economically competitive. Thus, it is increasingly difficult for parents to support their children's achievements by attending games, plays, and recitals. When they are unable to spend as much "quality time" with their children as they desire or think is required, they feel guilty about fulfilling their obligation to control—that is, regulate and discipline—their children.

Elkind also delineates two important shifts in family orientation toward parenting and childhood. The first shift is in what we see as the method of parenting, which, he argues, has shifted from an emphasis on intuition to an emphasis on technique. That is, modern parents are admonished to follow the prescriptive and structured advice given by experts on the child. The second shift is in our definition of childhood, which has changed from emphasizing innocence to emphasizing competence. When children were regarded as innocent, they were often left to their own devices to "play." Now children are expected to be competent, self-reliant, and autonomous. Adult-supervised competition is replacing the child's "play." Of course, as Elkind points out, streets and parks are no longer safe for unsupervised child's play, as they were several decades ago.

Professional Mothering

Though fathers are expected more and more to take an active role in the daily care and parenting of their children, the mothering role is still considered more crucial in the rearing of successful children. Most of the parental pressure falls on the woman, and it is the mother, especially the working mother, who suffers the severest and most enduring of the guilt trips. Today a significant proportion of mothers work full time, but the idea that mothering is a profession and women's highest calling dates to a period in our history when far fewer mothers worked and were relatively freer to pursue their "call."

Barbara Ehrenreich and Deirdre English have fully documented the development of the mothering role in the United States in their book *For Her Own Good*.[11] The turn of the twentieth century brought a scientific approach to childbearing, at a time in American culture when childhood itself began to stand out as a distinctive period of life. Gradually, children came to be regarded as the key to the country's future, and at the same time the image emerged that children were pliant and teachable. The "noble calling," then, of womanhood at that time was to raise and mold children capable of assuring the future of the United States (and this view persists in modified form today). As everything else in life was becoming scientific, so was motherhood; women were to rear their children properly, carefully, and rationally, according to the principles of science in general and the nascent psychological sciences in particular. This was the beginning of a long period, which *is still going on*, in which women are admonished to follow expert advice in rearing their children for success.

It is appropriate to ask whether parents, and especially mothers, have lost confidence in their natural parenting abilities. Christopher Lasch thinks so, and he contends that the vast amount of psychiatric and psychological advice available has not only undermined the confidence of parents but, more important perhaps, has also inflated the importance of child-rearing techniques and parents' responsibility for failure.[12] Lasch argues convincingly that parents today have few standards of their own for raising children and are left with only the children's peers against whom to judge and measure their children's academic and psychological development. Just as industrialization undermined and devalued the knowledge of craftsmen and workers in favor of the "scientific management" of the 1920s and 1930s, so the rise of the psychological sciences of child development devalued parental knowledge and ability and made them appear ineffective and unsophisticated. Ehrenreich and English would concur, but they contend that mothers caught most of the brunt of this, as their natural abilities to rear children were seen as inferior to the knowledge of the psychologist-expert. Moreover, the domination of the psychological sciences over mothering enabled men to use medical and scientific ideology to maintain their control of women.

Thus, today women are under considerable pressure to mother their children intensely so that the children can achieve and measure up, even as their natural abilities to mother are devalued and held suspect. Likewise, they must measure up to the performance standards of good mothering, or they fail themselves and their children. And women cannot seek a remedy to this quandary by looking within themselves, toward their own inner qualities and strengths; rather, like their counterparts of decades ago, they must place their fate and destinies as mothers in the hands of the friendly psychologist or helping professional.

Anthropologist Sheila Kitzinger uncovered a revealing contrast between mothering in American culture and mothering in peasant cultures.[13] In a peasant community, there are norms of mothering that remain unquestioned, and women do not feel subject to criticism because they just do what the women of the village have always done. By comparison, in our culture new mothers are continually bombarded by advice, from those who have had children and those who have not. Only in cultures such as ours, where conflicting advice abounds and women are required to seek it, can mothers experience failure in measuring up to motherhood norms. And only in such a culture do mothers anxiously "compare their products" to see if their children are keeping pace developmentally with other babies.

Parents Magazine, which once boasted a paid circulation of 1,500,000, is typical of an American magazine for parents (but I suspect that it is read mostly by women) that just teems with expert advice about rearing children. Parents can now get advice twenty-four hours a day over the telephone by dialing 1-900-680-KIDS. Although such a magazine would have little value for women in peasant societies, it is eagerly read by many women pressured to do things right as mothers. *Parents* leaves no child-rearing stone unturned; it is replete with expert/scientific knowledge, presented in question-and-answer columns, in guest articles, and in feature stories. For the past several years and in keeping with the model of child development, *Parents* has included an entire section, entitled "See How They Grow," devoted to demarcating the developmental stages: "As They Grow: Birth to One Year," "As They Grow: One Year Old," and so on. Each year of development is considered problematic; thus, a childcare expert (usually a psychologist, pediatrician, or psychiatrist) solves for the reading mother some problem she presumedly will have with her offspring at that age.

Consider a 1995 issue of *Parents* that gave advice to parents of two-year-olds on how to "Build Free Time into Your Child's Daily Schedule." Notice the implication that even two-year-olds have such "scheduled" lives that "free time" must be built in. Or consider the August 1995 issue, which contained an advertisement for Kinder Care that proclaimed: "Developing the child takes the whole day!" The ad went on to delineate the entire daily round of activities crucial to development provided by that day care organization. And even more poignant, in the December 1995 issue, in an article in the "Work and Family Life" column, we hear the guilt implicit in one working woman's story: "I never wanted to feel that Matt missed out on anything because I had to work," says Helen, a lawyer and mother of five-year-old Matt. "And if that meant getting up early Saturday morning for swimming lessons or going to an early evening art lesson with him I did it. I tried to make up for the time I was working by packing the time that Matt and I had together with all kinds of rich activities."[14]

School: Beyond Toddlerhood

The continuity of the measuring-up process for children and parents is assured by the public school system. Although children's lives include a series of arenas in which they are expected to prove themselves and show their potential, in no other arena is the performance ethic pursued with as much single-minded and vigorous commitment as in school. Living up to adult expectations on the Little League field is nothing compared to the pressures in the classroom, as most nine- and ten-year-olds soon discover.

David Elkind argues that modern education is no longer child centered but, rather, curriculum driven.[15] Whereas schools once were concerned with nurturing and supporting children, in this era of the "competent" child schools emphasize academic achievement as measured by grades and test scores. The responsibility is now passed to the teacher to prod, poke, size up, measure, and in many other ways encourage students to "succeed." And schools armed with a host of tests and other tools for measuring potential and gifts are more than adequately prepared for the task.

One of the underlying assumptions made by school authorities, particularly in the early grades, is that a child's transition from home to school will proceed smoothly if the mother has done her job in the home during the child's earliest years—that is, if the mother has intensely nurtured and prepared her child for school discipline and success by reading aloud and in other ways pruning the child's abilities and potentials as a kindergarten or first-grade student. Although parents are not expected to present a finished product to the kindergarten teacher, they are at the very least expected to have provided a home environment conducive to school success and to have inculcated in the child values that will make him or her teachable and competitive.

To ensure these smooth transitions and mother's continued support of measuring-up experiences, mothers are co-opted into PTA activities. That was the minimum requirement of a generation or two ago. Today, even working mothers of schoolchildren are cajoled into accepting roles as parent-sponsors of Brownies, Scouts, and a number of booster organizations from varsity athletics to band and choir. How many mothers of schoolchildren feel guilty when they must sidestep running for PTA office because they realize that work and other commitments simply prevent them from having the time? And how much stronger are the guilt feelings when these same mothers realize that many of the women who do volunteer for PTA office are just as pressured as they are?

One of the best pictures we have of this uneasy and sometimes anxious relationship between parents, children, and schools is presented in *Crestwood Heights*, by John Seely and his colleagues.[16] I recommend this remarkable study to anyone interested in the social life of a middle-class suburb, and though the research was carried out in Canada during the late 1950s, it sounds and feels very modern and close to home. Crestwood Heights (a fictitious name for a real community) was typical of the white-collar suburbs that sprang up throughout Canada and the United States during the economic expansion and prosperity of the 1950s. Seely and his associates discovered that Crestwood Heights was populated by young, upwardly mobile couples and parents who pursued the good life (that is, success, status, and material wealth) not only to satisfy themselves but to set a good example for their children. Thus, in Crestwood Heights there was an understood connection between good parenting and a good school system, and community norms encouraged, even required, the linkage. Parents were tied to the interests of the school system through the Home and School Association, a parent-school organization that was structured to keep the channels of communication open between parents and school authorities. Mothers, especially, were expected to be active in the Home and School Association, as a "good mother" was one who took a vital interest in her child's school life.

The two dominant values of Crestwood Heights were maturity and success, and these values not only permeated the school system but formed the ethos of the Home and School Association as well. This meant that schoolchildren were encouraged to be competitive (thus successful) yet cooperative and democratic in social relationships (as a sign of maturity). During Home and School Association meetings, parents were most interested in determining how well their own children were living up to the maturity and success values, particularly in relation to other children of similar age and grade. Parents were always pleased to learn that the school authorities shared similar concerns about how students were measuring up and could provide a variety of ways of assessing performance.

What was the effect of this on children? A good deal of pressure—and there was the rub. The children of Crestwood Heights were expected to live up to the contradictory features of the community culture. Especially in school, children were to be success oriented, striving for material wealth and high social statuses: *competitive yet cooperative!* And there was a further contradiction: Children were to gain a sense of maturity, whose values were expressed in various kinds of permissiveness. School authorities promoted the idea that children needed certain "freedoms" to make their own choices in life, for this was the essence of maturity, the wise exercising of options. Yet children in Crestwood Heights were heavily imbued with success values that required them to select those options that would maximize academic and vocational achievements. What masked as freedom for children was in reality a system of forced choices, selecting among competitive means to ensure eventual adult success.

Though the Home and School Association stressed a cooperative and mutually beneficial relation between parents and school officials, Seely's group concluded that the school was taking over more of the responsibility for childhood socialization and, in relation to parents, was *much* more certain of its methods. For example, at Home and School Association meetings, parents often asked for teachers' advice about rearing their children, to the point of asking what time their children should go to bed. All in all, Seely and his colleagues discovered that the school was looming ever larger in the lives of children and parents were assuming the roll of junior partners in preparing their children for adult success.

Let's take a closer look at how schools are becoming so heavily involved in the socialization of children by considering a primary-grade teacher and his or her charges. An interesting though not unexpected feature of education today, particularly at the primary level, is the infusion of the psychological sciences in education pedagogy. For instance, at my university, students majoring in elementary education are required to take two courses in psychology, and two additional psychology courses are strongly recommended as electives. No teacher in our society today is considered credible unless he or she is fully imbued with psychological theory, especially the models and concepts that emerge in a steady stream from educational and child development psychology.

Like most social and behavioral sciences, psychology has gained its academic prestige and cultural popularity and acceptance through its ability to measure things. Whatever the human trait, skill, competence, or yearning, some psychologist can measure and test for it. And not only that, he or she can tell how an individual ranks in relation to others. Psychology has become the preeminent behavioral science in academic and popular culture because in a performance-dominated society, psychology provides the ideological legitimation for our relentless measuring activities.

Nowhere is this more evident in our society than in the school systems, where education and learning are thought of almost exclusively in performance terms. "What is my child learning?" has pretty much come to mean "How well is my child performing?" We can hardly think of learning apart from performance because we lack the language to understand real learning. Schoolteachers are encouraged to speak the language of psychology, which means they tend to view learning solely in terms of measured academic performance. And this is another reason that parents have become junior or limited rather than full partners in their child's education. Despite all their exposure to their own psychological experts in raising their children, compared to teachers who have drunk heavily at the fountain of academic psychology, parents remain amateurs and "unprofessional." Thus, though parents are urged to be supportive and involved, they are expected to leave the "real teaching" of their children to professionals much better versed in the psychological sciences of growth, development, and learning.

In the classroom today, it is the psychologist who can scientifically inform the teacher what to expect from students, how to measure it, what the measurement "means," and, more significantly, how to correct deviations from the norm. Many examples could be given about the profusion of measurements in the classroom, but I will restrict my focus to standardized tests, the bane of so many children.

What started so innocently at the turn of the century with Alfred Binet's attempts to devise a scale to measure age-specific intelligence to identify retarded children has since produced a whole technology and industry of tests and scales, machine-graded and scored, and standardized for group norms, tests that now no worthy educational system can do without. Standardized tests of basic skills have not only hurried children through schooling but have created terrific pressure on pupils to perform early, often, and well. Test anxiety has trickled down to the primary-grade level.

And the anxiety of measurement is not only felt by school-age children but also increasingly by teachers and principals, who must satisfy school boards and other external groups that their students are indeed measuring up. Students' ability to score well on standardized tests is now the "measure" of good teaching and good administrating, as school districts compete with crosstown rivals to see which schools scored highest. As Elkind contends, such emphasis only serves to strengthen the factory-like quality of our schools, leading us to become obsessed with a measurable educational product and outcome. Moreover, teachers lose their sense of independent status as they become part of the "management systems" geared toward goal setting, scheduling, and monitoring class progress toward objective, measurable educational aims.

What passes for educational "reform" in many states is the implementation of ways to assure local corporations and tax boards that schools are in a quantifiable way more accountable. For example, in Indianapolis recently, a school reform bill supported by the mayor called for more staff performance evaluations, merit pay for teachers, and the publication of school performance statistics, that is, of statistics showing how students in different schools performed on standardized tests.

Thus, schools and their participants—teachers, pupils, and administrators alike—are under great pressure to perform well on each new batch of tests and scales to measure some kind of performance valued in the larger culture. No one denies that some of the abilities tested are of intrinsic value and importance in a technological and industrial culture. But when the tests themselves and the corresponding measurement scores are pursued for their own sakes, serve to dehumanize learning and learners, or create undue pressures for children to perform early and well, they can only do a disservice to real learning.

The same mania for standardized-test scores in reading and other skills characterizes our obsession with measuring the "intelligence" of our schoolchildren as a means of determining future learning potential. Happily, the worst excesses of intelligence testing are disappearing, but for decades schoolchildren were tested for intelligence early in their primary-grade career. Children who scored high were considered the brightest, more was expected from them, and they were often assigned to accelerated classes. Students with low scores were thought to be slow and were placed into groups where the teaching pace was slower. Over the years, the "bright" students showed accomplishment (surprise!), received better grades, pleased their teachers, and, with some exceptions, went on to high school or college. The slow students didn't do as well and were gradually and subtly shunted into vocational and practical courses; many would eventually drop out of high school. We know today that the difference between what the brighter students accomplished and what the slower students accomplished was due only in small part to real differences in ability. There is a **self-fulfilling prophecy**—that is, an expectation that comes about because it is expected—here: When teachers believe that a particular group of children are bright, they give them more attention and encouragement; they hold out high expectations, and the children tend to live up to them. The converse of this holds true for students who teachers feel are slow. The consequences are very real; the bright students tend to move onward and upward, and the slow ones tend not to. Yet what are the real differences in ability between the two groups? Probably not much. In our zeal to measure intelligence in some objective, numerical way, we have treated the "quotients" as if they were *real* and have placed children onto learning tracks that will to a considerable degree determine their life course in terms of high school diploma, college degree, career expectations, and so on.

Often differences in early test scores reflect differences in the social class background of the children being tested rather than variations in natural ability. Thus, working-class and lower-class children are usually at a disadvantage when required to show early ability on standardized tests. **School tracking,** arranging students by ability groups, is often a mirror of the community's social class and status divisions rather than the objective and scientific demarcations of students' natural ability. Appropriate here is my wife's experience as a student in a grade-school reading group. Her teacher had divided her class into two reading groups on the basis of early tests of reading skills. Her group, the Bluebirds, was an accelerated group, while the Redbirds was the slower-paced group. As a child, my wife was not altogether clear on the distinctions between the two groups, so that when her mother asked her one day if her group had the best readers, she answered, "I'm not sure. But our group wears the nicest clothes."

Putting aside the issue of class distinctions, any child who wants to do well in our society must measure up early; high scores are the name of the game in grade school. Today's children have not the leisure for early mistakes and failures. They had better not be too slow to develop and find themselves; they have little margin for error.

Yet we know (or should know) that intelligence and other human traits and capacities are so varied, multifaceted, and complex that to treat them as unitary variables that can be precisely measured and ranked is nearly ludicrous. So why do we persist? Why do we feel compelled to see our children as objects and to define their worth and value in terms of point scores, ratios, and quotients? Maybe early testing of children makes good science and good pedagogy, but why should parents go along with it so willingly and uncritically?

And I am not blaming any particular individuals; as the saying goes, some of my best friends are teachers, psychologists, and school officials. Most of them are well meaning and well intentioned, but they and we have permitted measurement mania, our cultural lust for measured, objective performance, to determine much of the school curriculum and much of what constitutes teaching. More significantly, the performance ethic in schools has led to an all-too-convenient labeling of ability and potential, not so much defining what a child actually *can* do or *be* as relying on what *tests* measure as ability or achievement. And on the basis of these scientific and objective tests, we have consigned some children to the more rewarding and honored callings of our society, while others who have come up short, however early in their careers, are eventually consigned to the lesser rewards of the lower rungs reserved for the "less able."

To what end is our preoccupation with testing children and pushing them to perform well in school directed? Can we have any assurance that what we are doing to our children in school is in any way promoting real learning or even enhancing a child's opportunities for success or creativity? Daniel Goleman, a Harvard-educated psychologist, answers this in his recent book *Emotional Intelligence.*[17] Goleman argues that the lives of many young people are fraught with problems because of emotional incompetence. Whether in the form of anger, depression, aggression, or even violence, uncontrolled and misunderstood emotions are the root of these young people's problems, in Goleman's view. Their failures are not the result of intellectual incompetence so much as of stunted and misguided emotional lives.

Since World War II our society has relied heavily on quantitative scores of intelligence and aptitude (SATs) to predict the future success of young people. But as Goleman demonstrates, we are discovering today that many intellectually competent people, such as valedictorians and persons with high IQs, do not always achieve success. Why? Because they cannot cope with the problems that life puts into their paths. A better predictor of one's future, according to Goleman, is one's emotional competence; one's ability to cope successfully with the inevitable pressures and stresses of life. What is **emotional intelligence?** Briefly, the ability to recognize and understand one's own emotions; to motivate oneself with a sense of optimism and hope; and to recognize and empathize with the emotions of other people. A person who is adept in these tasks is one who is emotionally competent and reasonably adjusted in life, and one who will do reasonable well.

Can emotional intelligence be precisely measured? Goleman would answer: not yet; maybe never. There are no paper-and-pencil tests that can be factored into an emotional "quotient." There are no comparative scores. And maybe that is the beauty of the idea of emotional intelligence. Goleman and others working in this area argue that emotional intelligence is a real and an important element in the life satisfaction of adults, adolescents, and children.

Another part of the good news here is that schools can be great training grounds for improving the emotional competence of young people. Although some persons are more naturally "gifted" emotionally than others, all persons are capable of improving and enhancing their emotional competencies. Teachers can, with the proper curriculum and school environment, teach young people to better understand, control, and deal with their emotions. Schools can do much more to ensure that emotional competence is considered to be as important as intellectual ability. Goleman is hopeful that soon the learning of emotions in schools will be on an equal footing with the learning of math, science, and language.

However, given that emotional competence cannot be measured quantitatively—and thus that students cannot be ranked and compared and that schools cannot be ranked and evaluated—it is possible, and perhaps probable, that grades and standardized tests will continue to be the essential measures by which learning is evaluated. Grades and test scores fit better the requirements of the performance culture, which still dominates our educational life.

We will return to some of Goleman's ideas about emotional competence in Chapter 3 as we look at the impact of the performance ethic on the lives of adolescents in the United States.

Key Terms

1. Apgar Score
2. The Serious Childhood
3. Intensive Parenting
4. Parkinson's Law of Parenting
5. Self-Fulfilling Prophecy
6. School Tracking
7. Socialization
8. Institutions
9. Taking the Role of the Other
10. Looking-Glass Self
11. Significant Others
12. Self as a Social Product
13. Emotional Intelligence

Review Questions

1. What did Philip Aries mean when he said moderns are "obsessed with the idea of childhood"?
2. In premodern society, which institutions had moral authority over children?
3. What role have the behavioral and medical sciences played in defining childhood and parenting today?
4. How and why are children's lives so structured and highly organized today? How is this related to the performance ethic?

5. What are some of the sources of parental guilt in our society?
6. In what ways can the mothering role in our society be seen as "professionalized"?
7. How do modern schools continue to promote the performance ethic started in the home?
8. Is school success always a predictor of future success? Why or why not?
9. What is "emotional intelligence"? How is it different from intellectual ability?

Discussion Questions

1. Reflect on your childhood. Do you feel that your life was unusually scheduled and organized? What role did organized sports, lessons, clubs, and organizations play in your childhood?
2. Did your parents have a concept of spending "quality time" with their children? Were your parents active in your developmental activities?
3. Reflect on your grade school days. How did you react to teaching, standardized testing, and grade pressure? Did you do well in these things? If not, how did you deal with it?
4. How might grade school education be reformed to make it less competitive and more nurturing?

Activities

1. Peruse some popular magazines for adults about family life (for example, *Redbook, Parents*). What sort of advice do they give? Who gives it? What do these magazines tell adults to be? Report your findings back to the class.
2. Interview some parents with young children. What are their problems in raising children? How do they get help? What counsel and advice do they rely on? Why? Report your findings back to the class.

3

Why Teens Try Harder: Adolescent Life in the United States

We continue our analysis of the measured self in this chapter devoted to examining adolescent life in our society.

Two sociological concepts, the reference group and impression management, will help us understand why and how adolescents are so concerned with their self-identity and their success in measuring up.

Reference groups are groups that a person can use to evaluate his or her own behavior.[1] It is from certain reference groups that we acquire a sense of who we are, where we stand, and whether our actions and behaviors are appropriate. We may belong to these reference groups or we may not. As a member of a football team or the student honor society, we might try to compare and adjust our actions in reference to our teammates or our classmates in the honor society. On the other hand, we may enjoy the music of a famous rock band and thus emulate the clothing styles, values, and behavior of some of the musicians in the band. In either case, football teams, honor societies, and rock bands are examples of reference groups that people can use to evaluate and compare their behavior. We know adolescence is a life stage in which a good deal of comparing and evaluating goes on. Young people are commonly concerned with where they stand, how they rank, how they look, and with whom they are seen. Reference groups provide the standards, norms, and values by which young people can compare themselves and others. As such, reference groups can exert a forceful influence on our actions and identities. Later in this chapter we will examine the appropriateness of some of the reference groups that many adolescents use to compare their behaviors and identities. Do some reference groups, for example, set standards of looks, body shape, or material wealth that are nearly impossible for many adolescents to emulate?

Impression management is a process closely linked to the concept of reference group. Sociologist Erving Goffman once argued that social life is like a stage upon which we are all actors trying to bring off a successful performance.[2] We do this by managing the impressions that others have of us. We want to look good on stage so that others will evaluate our performance positively. In Goffman's view, all we possess as actors in social life to give us a credible performance are our props, costumes (clothes), and images. Essentially, if we look good and are credible to others, then indeed we are good. Goffman has been accused of being rather cynical in this regard, for in this view only impressions count. Whatever we might think of Goffman's approach in general, we might agree that in our society impression management is a crucial undertaking for mos adolescents. "Coolness" in looks, dress, taste, and action is an impression that many young people work hard to create or manage. And conversely, no impression is more significantly damaged than that of a person regarded as nerdy, geeky, fat, or uncool. For adolescent life in our society is indeed a life stage in which impressions count, and how a young person manages his or her impressions is crucial to how he or she measures up in terms of popularity and acceptance.

*   *   *

Let's look now more closely at the measured self in the teenage and young adult years.

The genius of "Peanuts," one of the most widely read cartoon strips in the United States, lies in its uncanny ability to capture adult humor and pathos through the trials and tribulations of children. Not too long ago, a "Peanuts" cartoon featured Charlie Brown and Lucy seated on a couch as Charlie thumbed attentively through a catalog and lamented to Lucy, "These catalogs with their models are depressing! Everyone is handsome and beautiful! Look at them in their new spring clothes. It sets an impossible standard for us kids. None of us can ever grow up to look that good." Whereupon Lucy smiles smugly and announces: "I will."

Leave it to Lucy and her irrepressible personality and gall to dismiss Charlie Brown once again. Yet many children, adolescents, and young adults can surely feel and appreciate the significance of Charlie's fears.

"How," they worry, "can I grow up and meet the many standards the world has set before me? How will I become happy yet feel that I have in some or most ways measured up?"

In Chapter 2, following the work of historian Philip Aries, we learned that childhood as a special, demarcated time of life was a fairly late development in Western societies; it is probably only a few centuries old. I think a similar line of argument can be advanced in thinking about adolescent life in modern society. While the idea of childhood took several centuries to emerge in Europe, adolescence as a special period between childhood and adulthood is likewise very modern, with expressions such as "peer group" and "teenager" being generally accepted only within the past four decades.

My approach is to view adolescent life, in light of the performance ethic, as a stage of life infused with almost constant pressure on young people to measure up and to define their identities according to standards set by others. This measuring-up process, which begins in early childhood, continues unabated into adolescence as it magnifies and intensifies. Young women and men in our society gradually discover that much, perhaps all, of their social identity is fashioned from how well they have conformed to various performance standards that permeate adolescent life.

I think most critics would admit that many adolescents respond reasonably well to the variety of performance pressures. In a word, these young people have to cope with the demands by making identity and lifestyle adjustments. Indeed, to cope successfully becomes the hallmark of a well-adjusted teenager. And, like parents, the contemporary adolescent can turn to myriad magazines, books, and "how-to" manuals that sell advice, at affordable rates, on how to be a successful teenager. The messages are often slick and glib and are always upbeat and optimistic; the magazines are glossy and colorful.

One does not need to be a professional critic, however, to recognize that there is a dark side to adolescence that is often ignored or minimized. We are increasingly aware, despite our denials, that a significant and growing minority of young people do not cope very well in making satisfactory adjustments to performance pressures. A grim reminder of this fact was established recently by educators Charles Basch and Theresa Kersch, who in their study of adolescent stress pointed out: "Adolescents are the only age group for which mortality rates have increased in the recent past."[3] Moreover, this age group now experiences disproportionate rates of suicide, anxiety, accidents, and unwanted pregnancy.

Many would agree that the playful mirth of Lucy and Charlie Brown masks the uncomfortable reality that for a growing segment of our society's young people, the performance ethic is exacting a heavy toll. For a sizable number of adolescents, drug abuse, psychological anxiety, suicide, eating disorders, and running away have become all too common responses to failing to measure up.

Peer Paralysis

Sociologists define the **peer group** as a membership group of similar age and interests.[4] What is important, from the standpoint of socialization, is that the peer group is a company of equals. During the past few decades, much has been written and researched concerning the adolescent peer group and its extraordinary influence in the lives of young people. Most readers are now at least casually familiar with the findings of sociologists, psychologists, and social workers revealing that few teenagers in modern society "go it alone." To be isolated, apart, and alone is to become a virtual nonentity in the subculture of American adolescence. Perhaps the one condition most universally feared among adolescents is to be ignored by and isolated from an important peer group. At this stage of life, the need to belong is highly stimulated, and this need for group acceptance drives individual teenagers to accept the performance dictates of the group. To belong is to conform and to live up to the standards of the group, whether the standards are grades, looks, affluence, popularity, or whatever.

I'll argue that maturation in the adolescent stage means, in part, that young persons no longer require or seek the supervision and guidance of significant others, such as parents and teachers. It is during adolescence that the **generalized other,** a concept developed by Mead to describe the powerful, pervasive controlling effect of group life, becomes increasingly important.[5] In a sense, the generalized other refers to society and culture. Yet the effects of society and culture on individual conformity are normally mediated by smaller groups, such as families, peer groups, and organizations. For modern adolescents, participation in the peer group subculture is in reality learning to accept and live by the norms and values of the larger society. Of course, the peer group develops many norms, values, and standards of evaluation of its own, some of which are in harmony with those of the larger society and others not. Little of this is terribly conscious or highly organized except in the instances of clubs or delinquent gangs.

Within the peer group, each person is expected to internalize the standards of the group, to judge for him- or herself how well he or she is doing in measuring up to standards, and to apply corrections when necessary. On the surface, this all sounds like a growing maturity, what we might call "self judgment." The problem, however, is that very often the individual in the peer group does not question the appropriateness or suitability, to say nothing of the healthiness, of the group's norms and standards. Many young people find themselves trying to measure up to group standards and expectations at the expense of their personal morality, physical health, and psychological well-being.

Under these conditions we have **peer paralysis:** the inability, unwillingness, and even fear of young persons to think and be on their own apart from the group. When adolescents are paralyzed by the will of their peer group, they are not too likely to choose their own path, despite all the rhetoric in our society about human individualism. And, tragically, when adolescents do attempt to break out on their own, they often do so in harmful and even self-destructive ways.

Peer paralysis would not be possible, however, but for the fact that during adolescence young people learn not only to judge themselves but also to judge others. The latter, to be willing and capable of assessing others as well as oneself, is also part of a growing maturity. Whereas adults have become rather accustomed to their dual responsibilities as judge and judged, the nascent development of these capacities among teenagers can cause a good deal of anxiety.

Following this line of argument, my feeling is that adolescents "buy into" the performance ethic (many with a vengeance) despite the resulting anxieties that some of them experience. Teenagers and young adults soon find themselves inextricably mired in situations where they spend much of their time judging how well they are performing according to group standards and much of their time judging their peers.

One possible reason for the fact that teenagers have adequate time to dabble in the higher realms of peer evaluation is that, increasingly, they have little else to do. In contrast to children and preadolescents, whose time is filled with organized activities, teenagers are more on their own to develop the peer subcultures. And although contemporary high schools are somewhat demanding of the time and energy of their teenage students, they leave ample occasions for peer group life to emerge and solidify. The more vocal critics of public education contend that many high schools do little more than "teen sit" for busy working parents. While I would agree with this assessment in part, I don't think the modern high school and its administrators and teachers are entirely responsible. The issue becomes a bit more complex when we take into account the pronounced changes in the U.S. economy of the last few decades.

The shifts and dislocations of our industrial and technical economy have resulted in a society in which there are far fewer employment opportunities for adolescents and young adults, at least the kind that pay well, provide upward career mobility, and garner prestige. I'm not referring to jobs behind the counter and at the drive-in window at McDonald's. In an effort to hold down unemployment rates and to parcel out the available better-paying jobs to adults, the entrance of thousands of young people into the labor force must be delayed. Although few teachers and administrators would care to admit it, the U.S. high school serves this function rather nicely.

Modern students find themselves enduring four years of high school in which the academic requirements, though somewhat rigorous, rarely tax the ability of the average student. Academic standards can hardly be made more difficult since high schools are under pressure to keep teenagers off the street and out of both the employment and unemployment lines. It is worth noting, of course, that in the suburban high school, and within certain peer groups, obtaining superior grades is a source of considerable and intense measuring-up pressure. One cannot minimize the importance of grades among the upwardly mobile, middle-class, and professional parents or the pressures they exert on their children.

In general, though, adolescent life and the high school setting provide sufficient time and opportunities for the formation of peer groups and their subsequent paralyzing effects on individualism. The peer group becomes the mediating arena for all sorts of measuring-up activities and provides countless opportunities for young persons to set standards and judge performances.

It is important, though, that we realize that the various performance standards of the peer group are not developed in a social vacuum. This could hardly be the case in the United States, where the relentless quest for capitalist profit often provides the impetus for social standards and expectations. The peer performance world itself is quite vulnerable to Madison Avenue influence. As many entrepreneurs of adolescent fads and fashion realize, there is a good deal of money to be made in marketing products—music, styles, and gadgetry, for example—to teenagers. While Madison Avenue busily creates the need and the adolescent peer culture provides the group pressure, young people in our society live in a virtual counterculture of measurement, a counterculture in which their identities are assessed and defined by the cars they drive, the clothes they wear, the music they listen to. And this whole process is fueled by magazines catering exclusively to teenagers, providing myriad advertising images for them to look to in search of the measured self. In a heavily materialistic society such as our own, of all the bases on which adolescents can choose to judge themselves and others, nothing succeeds quite so well as commodities: things bought and sold in the teenage marketplace. Adolescents soon find the measured self within a **commodified identity**, an identity in which their sense of personal worth, of value, and even of selfhood is determined not by who they are but by what they can purchase, put on, listen to, or drive. It is within visible material fashions and lifestyles that the sense of self emerges and flourishes. But it remains a comfortable identity only insofar as the peer group continues to endorse the ultimate value of commodities.

The pressures on today's adolescent to measure up can often become contradictory. Especially for middle-class adolescents, the requirement to perform well academically must be balanced with the pressure to participate successfully in the hedonistic subculture, that is, the activities surrounding popular music, parties, having fun, dating, and "being seen" that teenagers are expected to enjoy and take part in. Though I refer to these activities as "hedonistic," there is a serious, subconscious dimension to them. Young people cannot ignore having fun and being cool. There are standards of taste, style, and conduct that are rigidly enforced and that teenagers must conform to. The individual teenager who desires to belong can neither ignore the standards nor hope to easily substitute his or her own.

Middle-class adolescents must keep one eye on their future college career, in the hopes of getting into the right school, and the other eye on how well they are performing in the world of coolness, fun, and fashion. Being able to achieve at a superior level academically may be possible only at the expense of complete and successful performance in activities after school and on weekends. How can one be admitted to the best universities after high school to launch a professional career yet be popular, accepted, well-rounded, and considered fun to be with while still in high school?

The domains I am about to elaborate are certainly not the only performance arenas; some readers will no doubt think of others. But I feel that the arenas I have chosen are crucial and should give us some insight into the nature of the measured self in adolescence. The performance domains that follow are actually broadly based societal pressures that do not necessarily originate in the adolescent subculture, but they are mediated, shaped, enforced, and given unique meaning within the workings of the peer group. To some degree, adolescents are living up to pervasive cultural mandates of U.S. society. Yet the forms of their striving, and its meaning for their lives, are to be understood within the specific context of the group processes that define adolescent life.

Looks: "Mirror, Mirror, on the Wall"

A young woman from Holland, an exchange student at the university where I teach, recently commented to one of her professors concerning a puzzling aspect of American culture: "I can't believe that American girls spend a half hour putting on makeup to go jogging!" Puzzling perhaps to a visitor from Holland but easily believable and understandable to those of us familiar with the importance of "looks" in our culture.

Though the pressure on males to be physically attractive is real, it is the adolescent female who faces the most severe performance pressure to look good and to make attractiveness a virtue. The adolescent female must develop a passion for her looks, a passion that is readily and continually stimulated by teenage magazines such as *Seventeen* and *Teen*. Even a cursory glance at these magazines is sufficient to understand the enormous concern generated by the advertisements about the importance of good looks. Virtually every page of a teenage magazine is filled with pictures of young women with perfect gleaming teeth, full-bodied, stylish hair, unmarred complexion, and an ideally shaped face and figure; each of them is dressed in the latest styles. And the subtle message conveyed to the young female reader is that she too can look like that if she tries hard enough or wants it badly enough, which of course she should. As might be expected, accompanying every picture of the perfect adolescent looks are the products—designer jeans, cosmetics, shampoos, rinses, acne medicines—products touted as being indispensable in helping the teenager create *the* image. What self-respecting adolescent female can reject such imagery and the magic allure of the commodities, especially if admission to certain peer groups requires the kind of looks that at least approximate the ideal? Maybe she will never look exactly like the model in the picture, but at least she can try if she wants to be popular.

Thus adolescents learn two things about their lives from the latent messages conveyed by teenage magazines: first, one must have the looks if one is to be popular and datable; second, commodities are necessary to acquire the looks. An acceptable self is purchasable; selfhood becomes a "thing," a market image. The pursuit of an identity has less to do with the recognition of inner qualities and more to do with an external commodified self that is thought to be within the grasp of those with sufficient money and best taste.

Complementing the obsession with looks is the adolescent's preoccupation with body imagery. Here again the strivings are most acute among teenage women, who become as concerned with their figures as with their faces. The American mania for feminine thinness that drives so many adult women to health spas, dieting centers, and diet magazines also permeates the adolescent world, where the obsession with thinness assumes cultlike qualities. The concern with slimness as a way of measuring up in the adolescent subculture often leads directly to eating disorders among women, with tragic psychological and physical consequences.

Within the adolescent world, physical appearance often forms the basis of status groups that take on characteristics of subcultures. Such groups become virtually castelike in that once a young person is affixed to a looks status group, there is hardly any escaping or crossing to another group. Those excluded from the status groups, most recognized within the high school setting, take on names like "jocks," "nerds," and "geeks," and both inclusion and exclusion from such groups are based on surface characteristics like body build, clothing style, and physical attractiveness, as well as on coolness in behavior.

Sociologically, we can witness here the power of the **labeling process,** the assignment of statuses and attributes. For once a young person becomes labeled as a "nerd" or "geek" or "greaser," it becomes exceedingly difficult for him or her to overcome the often devastating effects of the label on personal identity and social interaction within the school setting. As an example, a young man labeled as a greaser might soon be cut off from the kind of social interactions necessary to do well academically or athletically and might find himself forced to "live up" to the label. The label becomes a self-fulfilling prophecy that may result in a series of bad grades, a truancy record, and perhaps being dropped from school altogether. Membership in or exclusion from peer subgroups based on looks can severely hamper the academic success of many young people whose looks fail to measure up. Virtually all teenagers learn this upon entering high school, and thus they become conscious of their own appearance, knowing that to be otherwise jeopardizes admission into the favored status groups and threatens academic performance. This very attitude, however, only serves to reinforce the reality and validity of the status group and further enables the labeling process to flourish. Adolescents unwittingly create the very structures and processes that they fear and that restrict their individualism and freedom.

Getting the Grades

Though I argued earlier that high schools are not necessarily academically rigorous, middle-class youth cannot be satisfied merely to graduate and make average grades. Admission into prestigious and selective universities requires a superior academic record, and middle-class students must achieve high grades while taking the most challenging courses. These students can be in the uncomfortable position of having to do well academically but not in a way that compromises their popularity. The teenage daughter of one of my colleagues was studying one evening for an important exam in biology. This particular unit covered human reproduction. At one point the daughter interrupted her concentration and remarked to her mother, "It would be awful to fail . . . but, you know, it would be worse if I got everything right!"

Earning superior grades and garnering academic honors are important performance obligations for middle-class high school students for several reasons. To begin with, middle-class adolescents are under considerable pressure to please their parents, who want their children to do well academically as a demonstration that they are worthy of the thousands of dollars soon to be invested in their college education. Also, parents are beginning to realize at this stage that they are rapidly losing the tight control over their children that they have exercised for many years. Middle-class parents desire this last sacrifice to their dwindling authority.

Good grades are also important among middle-class adolescents as part of the requirements for general popularity and acceptance into certain peer groups. In suburban high schools, which contain predominately students from professional and middle-class backgrounds, superior grades and academic accomplishment are often the criteria for admission to the exclusive and prestigious peer groups. When this situation occurs, it is not surprising that parents encourage peer group life for their children as a reinforcement of their own wishes.

In U.S. society, for the middle and professional classes success means graduating first from a reputable university and then from graduate-level business or professional school. Though success might not be guaranteed by a college degree, in the minds of the middle class career success is hardly possible without it. The most selective of these colleges and universities set stiff academic barriers for admission, and aspiring high school students must measure up if they hope to be admitted.

Educational consultant Jan Krukowski's survey of high school students found that students identified a college as the "right" college according to what they perceived as the success of that college's graduates.[6] The more successful a particular college's graduates, the more the students considered that college to be right for them and the greater their willingness to get the grades required for admission. Thus, many contemporary middle-class high school students create their own academic pressures because they fear that high school mediocrity (let alone failure) will deny them entrance to the kinds of universities they see as so instrumental to future success.

David Elkind puts academic achievement in the category of what he calls Type C stress situations: those that are foreseeable but not avoidable.[7] Elkind contends that for many adolescents, academic achievement has replaced the deep interaction with peers and adults in which young people traditionally learned their manners and conduct codes. Consequently, academic success has become directly linked to self-esteem. Definitions of self-worth and personal value are tied to test scores and grades. Young people who do well in school are more confident of their self-worth and esteem; conversely, those whose academic achievements fall short of expectations see themselves in a less favorable light and develop a poor self-image. Elkind finds that when students begin to worry about tests, they can become angry at teachers for giving them and at parents for insisting their children study. Such students can develop cynical attitudes toward the school system. When academics become the basis for self-esteem, a student's every setback or shortcoming is a personal affront and takes something from his or her selfhood. Young people are sensitive to this situation yet powerless to change the process. Is it any wonder that they come to resent their schools, teachers, and parents? And this dynamic occurs in many adolescents who do well academically. Even the best students often experience alienation from their teachers because they realize the power of the grade to influence how others will think about them and, more important, how they will regard themselves.

The Sporting Life

Traditionally the world of competitive athletes has been a male domain where young men were expected to prove their mettle and test their manhood in competition. Over the past few years, however, we have witnessed a virtual explosion of interest in women's athletics, and in most high schools there is a significant number of young women trying to measure up on the basketball courts and baseball diamonds.

Competitive sports and the school system have worked hand in glove for many decades. We can hardly think of them separately. Athletics originally were viewed as a healthy outlet for students to work off the pent-up energy that resulted from sitting at desks for several hours on end. Sports were considered a healthy diversion, especially for males, who were thought to have the most energy to expend. High school athletic competition today is anything but an outlet and diversion, as school corporations find themselves financing expensive athletic programs. Insurance coverage for football teams alone can become a healthy chunk of the school's budget.

Moreover, the success of many a school administrator rests on his or her ability to hire winning coaches; no principal can take pride in being the doormat of the athletic conference. Schools are often evaluated according to the success of their athletic programs, and student athletes must perform well in competition for the sake of the school and the coach's job. Ironically, the athlete is expected to give his or her all for the honor of the same institution that during the school day administers all those detested exams!

The meaning of athletic competition in U.S. society, though, goes deeper than the mere measure of a school district's success. Competition is at the very core of the U.S. economic system, and successful athletic competition is linked strongly to the values of economic success. At every athletic awards banquet (college as well as high school), the student athletes are reminded that the lessons learned in sports are the same ones necessary for occupational success and career achievement. Hard work, self-discipline, the will to win, and teamwork are the hallowed values necessary for both a football victory and a healthy return on corporate assets. The captain of the basketball team is extolled as being only a few years removed from being a captain of finance. And just as the battle of Waterloo was said to have been won on the playing fields of Eton, so are the successes of corporate mergers and leveraged buyouts said to be achieved on the football fields of U.S. high schools.

The recent surge of interest in women's athletics in high school and college is tied to women's increasing participation in the corporate world. If the new women in management are to be effective team players, they too must learn the lessons of teamwork in athletic competition, and there is no better place to begin than in high school or even in the lower grades.

Though it is virtually heretical in our society to criticize high school athletic competition, one can still ask whether too much pressure is placed on young athletes to be "winners," to risk life and limb for a successful program. So-called amateur athletics at many Division I universities—where players are paid, where academic standards are severely compromised in recruiting, and where any number of student athletes don't even graduate—are more than preparation for big business; they *are* big business. Will we be able to say the same soon about high school sports, and will the pressure there on student athletes to save the school budget, the principal's honor, and alumni prestige parallel the situation at the college level?

Teamwork itself has many positive dimensions, but can excessive concern with athletic teamwork at the high school level exacerbate the pressure of the peer group that adolescents already feel so strongly? Young people in high school, as we have seen, are preoccupied with the fear of letting down the peer group. Might athletic competition become simply another arena where the fear of failing one's peers can loom large and where losing represents something deeper than scoring fewer points than the opponent? Under the pressure of living up to the expectations of teammates, coaches, parents, and school officials, just how free are today's young student athletes to fail, to lose, and to admit that their play is only a game?

The SAT: The Future as Guesswork

Another component of the performance ethic permeating adolescent life is the standardized testing so commonplace in determining who will go to college and where. For middle-class youth, this aspect of the performance ethic is especially keen; their chances of getting into the right colleges depend heavily on their scoring well on the SATs and the ACTs developed by the Educational Testing Service (ETS).

SAT exams have become a ritual in high schools. They are as entrenched as if they were decreed by divine authority. Students, school administrators, parents, and college admissions officers alike have accepted the SAT exams as a valid and fair part of the determination of who gets into which colleges. Students aspiring to be admitted to the "better" colleges and universities, however, come to view the taking of the SAT with a sense of dread, knowing that how well they score influences not only their collegiate futures but their sense of self-worth and their status in the peer groups to which they belong. For many middle-class students, taking the SAT has become a rite of passage.

Those who have misgivings about the undue emphasis on SATs in high school are indebted to author David Owen for exposing the workings of the ETS, which devises, administers, and scores a host of standardized exams.[8] The ETS is a tax-exempt corporation that generated $130 million in revenues during 1983, paying its officers handsome salaries to work in plush offices and impressive surroundings. Officials at ETS like the idea that positions in our society should be determined by scores on multiple-choice exams. They feel that superior and inferior ability can be scientifically measured. (Admittedly, SAT exams now include some essay questions.)

Owen reasons that ETS is a powerful and yet unregulated monopoly determining the fates of thousands of people who have no option but to take their tests and live by the scores if they want to be admitted to a certain college, law school, or graduate program. ETS assumes a gatekeeping function, letting some in and keeping others out depending on how they measure up on a series of multiple-choice questions administered on a certain morning.

David Owen's book levels devastating and deserved criticism at ETS, and I shall not go into it at length here other than to point out that test questions on the SAT are *not* necessarily developed by experts. Questions only need to be statistically reliable to be used. Nor are SAT scores a good predictor of college freshman grades, having a successful prediction rate of about 0.52 at best. Actually, SAT scores correlate quite nicely with family income: The higher the family income, the higher the SAT on the average. More important, perhaps, is Owen's contention that no official at ETS could tell him with any kind of exactness what "aptitude" really is. Yet the test scores supposedly measure it precisely. We can only conclude that the SAT scores really form a mystique, and unfortunately for many young people, a powerful one.

This mystique is so powerful, in fact, that most high schools that want to do right by their middle-class students now offer SAT preparation courses. Students who feel pressured to score high on their SATs find themselves enrolling in these courses, spending time they could have given to reading, doing homework, taking part in a drama or musical. And the gist of these courses is to teach students how to take multiple-choice exams: They teach not content or knowledge of a subject matter (let alone an appreciation of it) but how to eliminate the incorrect choices from among four or five given.

Of course, for families with money there are always expensively packaged programs available for private SAT tutoring. Many parents are quite willing to spend hundreds of dollars to see to it that their son or daughter measures up—after all, admission to the right college depends on it.

Over the past year or two, some of my students have been willing to share with me the pressures and anxieties they endured as high school seniors in getting admitted to the university where I teach. One of my students, Colby, comes from an affluent family living in a prosperous suburb of a large city, and he agreed to share parts of his diary with me. Colby appears to be a laid-back young man, his attire normally casual, loose-fitting, but expensive preppie garb. During his senior year in high school, his life was anything but casual and relaxed. Though he was a good high school student, Colby has the misfortune of having two older brothers whose high school grades were superior to his own. The same was true of his college board scores: They were not too bad, but they lagged behind his older brothers' scores. Colby's mother was displeased with this and required an evening study schedule for him. He was to spend two hours nightly exclusively on SAT preparation. His two older brothers had SAT scores high enough that they encountered no difficulty being admitted to elite Eastern colleges. Colby had a lot to live up to, as his mother reminded him one morning some months later. Before he left to take his SAT exams, she said, "Remember how your brothers did, Colby. We expect the same from you. Don't let us down. You don't want to stay at home and go to a junior college, do you?"

It is my feeling that SATs and similar standardized exams are tyrannizing many young people, even those students who have done well in their school courses only to come up short on a set of multiple-choice questions. Nevertheless, educational leaders continue to equate high SAT scores with real ability and educational aptitude, despite the fact that the SAT has little predictive value.

Daniel Goleman discovered an interesting thing about college SAT scores.[9] He found that hope was a stronger predictor of college success than the SAT. Moreover, the ability to motivate oneself and to control one's emotional life were also strongly related to academic success. The virtue of qualities such as hope, emotional control, and self-motivation is that these emotions can be nurtured and encouraged within the college setting. They may not be easily quantifiable, as scholastic aptitude supposedly is, but they are traits students can develop and change. Students can, with the help of the university, take some control over their emotional life as a way of enhancing their academic success.

As a university professor with over twenty-five years' experience, I am encouraged by Goleman's findings. The qualities I seek in a college student cannot be measured on an SAT, and perhaps they are not measurable at all. What I look for is a love of learning and knowledge, a curiosity about the world, and a willingness to risk something of oneself in order to learn. Through the years, I have taught many students with high SAT scores who do well on exams but who have little interest in the world of knowledge and ideas, whose curiosity is nearly nonexistent, and who take few, if any, risks. These students, and they are perhaps the majority, want a safe education, a secure future, a marketable major, and a lucrative career. Such persons are all too comfortable with the measured self, and I wonder if this is now becoming the standard "product" of an educational system that places so much emphasis on quantitative measures of aptitude and even learning itself.

This may well be the case in an era of fiscal accountability that extends even to institutions of education. States are now finding that their legislatures are willing to augment an educational budget only if the results are measurable. Thus, school systems will be pressured all the more to administer standardized, quantitative tests to students (sometimes even to teachers) to determine how much students have achieved academically, how ready they are for employment, and how cost-effective the teachers and administrators have been. In a society that measures all success by the bottom line, there is a tendency to judge education by the same standards and seek only, or at least primarily, those results that can be measured and compared. In the scramble for scarce funds, the losers will be determined by the numbers.

But is that what real learning is about? Will an educational system based on the corporate-quantitative-accountability model provide the best education for young people? Are the only things worth knowing those that can fit standardized multiple-choice exams? And, more important, in an era that virtually cries for creative and resourceful solutions to problems, can the ability to score high on standardized exams provide the kind of leadership we need so desperately?

And what of the lives of adolescents, whose opportunities for learning, increased self-awareness, and knowledge are sacrificed in favor of developing abilities to score well on exams administered once a year? How will these young men and women value real learning when they realize that much of their self-esteem and educational experience is represented by a single numerical score?

"Thin to Win"

As I pointed out earlier, adolescents are often overly concerned with body imagery. For males, the athletic, muscular build is a popular ideal; for females the ideal is the thin figure. On the surface it appears that males are getting off easier than females, because the athletic build is usually obtainable through moderate weight lifting, participation in sports, exercise, and so on. There is mounting evidence, however, that some young men are resorting to the use of anabolic steroids, often illegally obtained, to build more rapidly the kind of body associated with male heroes.[10]

Whereas some of the young men want bulk, most adolescent women desire thinness, and it is the relentless quest for thinness that all too often leads to eating disorders. Anorexia and bulimia are widespread in high schools and universities in the United States. The cultural ideal of feminine thinness promotes personal distortion and destructiveness. In this cultlike fascination with thinness, many young women are pushed over an emotional edge into the deep psychological disturbance associated with anorexia.

In an interesting study of cultural standards of feminine beauty, psychologist D. M. Garner and colleagues collected data from *Playboy* magazine.[11] They were particularly interested in the weight and measurement statistics of the centerfold models in the 1960s and 1970s. Not surprisingly, their research documented a shift toward the thinner figure. They found the same trend toward thinness in the measurement data for the women in the Miss America Pageants. However, and here's the rub, actuarial statistics reveal that in the population as a whole the average female build for those under age thirty actually got heavier in the same time period.

Here, then, we have the kind of dilemma so commonplace in societies where cultural ideals and expectations are out of line with human reality and need. While the models who pose for magazine centerfolds are getting thinner, women in the general population are becoming heavier, creating a tension in young women that is accompanied by pressure to diet. Is it any surprise that as the ideal of thinness permeates the adolescent world, most high school females are dissatisfied with their figures and want to diet or already are dieting? How else can they measure up?

Feminist Susie Orbach contends that watching what they eat has become second nature to many women as they try to adhere to the ideal of thinness.[12] Orbach also believes that most women don't question the ideal; they only feel bad when they fail to meet it.

Marlene Boskind-Lodahl has had much clinical experience treating adolescent anorexia and bulimia, and she believes that, contrary to what psychoanalytic theory claims, anorexic women have not rejected the feminine stereotype; rather, they have embraced it all too strongly.[13] Their obsession with thinness causes them to accept the feminine ideal in a very exaggerated form. Boskind-Lodahl argues that anorexics want to please men as a validation of their self-worth. When they experience rejection (real or perceived), their self-worth is damaged and an eating disorder ensues. Adolescent anorexics are often high achievers who get good grades in school, not as a personal goal but primarily to please others or to attract a man.

From a feminist perspective, Boskind-Lodahl believes that young women are socialized in our society to seek love from and eventual marriage with men. This is a woman's purpose in life. However, teenage women don't obtain the rewards they have been socialized to expect (love and marriage) because they are too young and because they are increasingly pressured to postpone serious courtship in favor of education. On a psychological level, then, trying to please men is a nearly impossible task for adolescent females, and those young women who try and fail are often those whose sense of self-worth is seriously damaged. Alternatively, this ruined self-concept can result in excessive dieting and binge eating to create the "worthy" figure.

Though by no means do all adolescent women become anorexic in the quest for thinness, too many do, and too many others, though not subject to eating disorders, are unhappy and frustrated trying to live up to an ideal that cannot be theirs or that cannot even bring them the satisfaction they hope for.

Popular media such as television, movies, and magazines also create an unrealistic standard of attractiveness for young people. When female adolescent reference groups for beauty include the cast of *Baywatch* or *Melrose Place,* a nearly impossible standard for body shape becomes the norm. *People* magazine recently explored the dilemmas faced by young women and even young men in trying to match their body shapes and sizes to the ideal set by Hollywood stars and supermodels.[14] In the world of fashion, television, and movies, only the superthin are hired and casted. Full-figured models and actors need not apply.

Adolescents are caught up in dieting fads as they try to emulate ultra-thin superstars, who themselves are nearly half-starved keeping their careers afloat. As a result, more and more teenagers are dissatisfied with their appearance. According to a poll conducted for *People* magazine, 45 percent of teenage females had negative feelings about their appearance one or more times a week. Even young males are becoming self-conscious about their body image. Ten percent of teenagers with eating disorders now are boys. And high school males are now reluctant to take showers after their gym classes, perhaps a further indication of their uneasiness with body imagery. However, young men are still more comfortable with their body image than are young women. Adolescent females are twice as likely to be dissatisfied with their body imagery than are young males. Is it any wonder that the diet industry generates 33 billion dollars in revenues annually? And according to *People* magazine, few Hollywood directors, producers, or actors are happy about this obsession with thinness. Casting directors would like to hire the most talented rather than the most nearly emaciated. But no one knows where to begin to make inroads on our culture's fascination with and adulation of the superthin.

Life and Death Matters

Adolescent suicide has entered the public consciousness with reports of copycat suicides and death pacts. Much of adolescent suicide can be linked to the deleterious pressures on young people to conform to impossible and contradictory standards. Yet there are tendencies to cover up and ignore what our culture is doing to young people and to lay the problem at the doorstep of the media by arguing that publicity about teenage suicide prompts other young people to take their lives as a means of gaining recognition and attention. Ignoring the reality of a problem, blaming its symptoms on publicity, is an old and familiar tactic in the United States. We used it to deny the importance and pervasiveness of public demonstrations and protests in the 1960s, arguing that those young people wouldn't be protesting if television cameras weren't rolling and reporters weren't there to interview them. This type of thinking fits nicely with what sociologist Philip Slater calls the "Toilet-Assumption" about social problems in U.S. society.[15] We don't want to face up to the problems created by certain of our cultural values, in the same way we don't want to live with excrement. By putting our social problems out of sight, just as we flush away excrement, we don't have to live with them; we can ignore their existence and refuse to deal with them, at least in any realistic and meaningful way.

Unfortunately (or maybe fortunately) this tactic will not work with adolescent suicide, and no amount of publicity can either cause or eliminate the problem. The fault is not in our coverage but in our culture, however reluctant we are to face that possibility.

Evidence on adolescent suicide shows it increasing sharply in the United States between 1960 and 1980, then leveling at a high rate.[16] In 1990, the adolescent suicide rate stood at 13.2 per 100,000. Among young people, suicide is often contemplated if not actually carried out. According to an Institute of Medicine study, even among students with high grades, one-third reported that they had considered suicide.[17] Also, 15 percent of high school students admitted to at least one suicide attempt.

There are many studies of adolescent suicide from several points of view, and I shall not review them here. However, I think we can safely argue that substantial numbers of young people attempt to take their own lives because their sense of self-worth is severely tarnished or destroyed. Such young people feel that their lives are ruined and hopeless. They have tried to measure up to the cultural ideals accompanying their roles as students, males, females, friends, and so on, and they have perceived rejection or failure. This, combined with the loss of supportive social structures to be found in family, peers, church, or neighborhood, generates the sense of loneliness and isolation leading to the formation of a death wish.

In his classic work *Suicide,* pioneer sociologist Emile Durkheim maintained that the breakdown of social norms and values associated with the emergence of industrial civilization often cast people adrift morally. Many would experience **anomie**, acute anxiety due to the overwhelming number of choices to be made without sufficient guidelines to make them.[18] One type of anomie (from the Greek "anomos," literally, "lack of meaningful order") is associated with the fact that most middle- and upper-middle-class people are socialized, particularly in adolescence, to believe that they can be anything they want to be, if only they "try hard enough."

Constantly forced to compare themselves with their peers athletically, socially, academically, and in other ways, the vast majority of adolescents necessarily find themselves coming up short. Despite the cultural rhetoric that "the sky's the limit," most young people's actual accomplishments necessarily and inevitably run up against the real limits on their natural abilities, looks, and so on. Moreover, even if they are especially able, the fact is that only one or two persons can be captain of the football team, there are only a limited number of places on the cheerleading squad, and valedictorians come only one to a graduating class. Despite these facts, young people, regardless of their actual levels of accomplishment, are always measured against a norm of perfection, often reiterated by their parents. Faced with such pressures, relatively privileged young people can and do develop negative self-images that, in extreme cases, can lead to depression and even suicide.

Even working-class youth, who have failed to measure up to even the minimal standards of academic performance by dropping out of school, are transforming personal failure into group tragedy. Witness the shattering effects of a suicide pact in Bergenfield, New Jersey, in which four "deeply troubled" youths took their own lives.[19] Three of the youths were high school dropouts. Estranged in various ways from their families, they belonged to an outcast group known as the "burnouts." Rejected by the more popular peer groups, having failed in the eyes of school authorities, this tiny group gave up their lives together rather than endure the feelings of worthlessness and loss of self-esteem so vital to people of their age.

How many lives will it take before we realize the devastating effects of the performance ethic and begin to recognize its pernicious influence among some of the most vulnerable of our people?

College Life and Late Adolescence

For some time now I've been impressed (not favorably) with the way the college experience has contributed to the measured self and by the way the college setting permits performance pressures nearly as severe as the peer culture of the middle teenage years. Since hundreds of thousands of young people in our society attend college, these performance pressures are worth looking at more closely.

What could the college experience be if we were to pursue the ideal of so-called higher education? "Higher learning" could be a respite from measurement and performance pressure; after all, one possible definition of university life is that of a community of scholars joining together to create, to understand, and to share knowledge. Ideally, the community would encourage a meeting of minds in which the younger scholars seek the wisdom and insight of the older, more experienced ones in a quiet, gentle, accepting environment where love for truth and knowledge is revered above all. Freedom to pursue the truth would be an essential priority. Moreover, students and professors alike would be drawn to the community because they share the same devotion to truth and knowledge.

Does this sound like the kind of university that most college students in the United States attend? With some notable exceptions among the most prestigious and academically oriented colleges, I would have to say no. This is not to say, however, that within a good many universities there isn't a segment of teachers and students trying to create the kind of community I've described. The problem is that they are in the minority, and in their darker moments, they know it. While nonuniversity people often refer to college campuses as "ivory towers," that is not a very accurate description anymore. (Some academics would argue that it never was.) College life is rarely impervious to the demands of the world, even the tawdry ones, and instead of providing a respite from the measured performance that dominates contemporary life, the college experience is largely an extension of it. The typical campus is rapidly becoming a setting in which few participants can avoid the measured self, as the identities of students and professors are shaped and given form by how well they measure up to a variety of standards, only a few of which have anything at all to do with love of knowledge and truth.

Most students find this out quickly. They learn the message even as high school seniors when they discover how intently interested college admissions officers are in their class rank, GPA, and SAT scores. They also become aware that to be admitted to the college of their choice it is these quantitative measures that are most closely scrutinized by admissions officers and that may ultimately determine the bottom-line judgment. If students were privy to these sessions, they would also learn that when college admissions officers really want to impress the faculty with the quality of the freshman class they have admitted, they often do so by citing their average SAT scores. A few thousand freshmen are categorized and evaluated by a pronouncement such as, "Their average verbal is 580 and that's up a few points." The faculty, particularly those in the English department, usually roar their approval.

Colleges play the numbers game with each other as well. *Time* magazine discovered in 1995 that many colleges manipulate and "massage" their SAT scores to look good, that is, not only to look selective to prospective students but to get favorable ratings in college guidebooks.[20] The quantification of aptitude can create a climate of deceit even among elite colleges and universities.

For those in late adolescence and within the university setting, peer paralysis is not nearly so great. But there remains the performance pressures of grades, choosing the right Greek living unit, selecting a major that will please parents, and being popular enough to get dates. In fact, it's my impression that the competitive, evaluative, and achievement pressures are as severe in the university environment as anywhere in society; many, if not most, students see in their college experience an opportunity to prove themselves worthy and acceptable for the career they hope to launch upon graduation. I've had more than one student say to me that when they graduate they hope that the curriculum they selected and the experiences they had would make them "pretty marketable."

Human Capital

Parents of today's college students exert significant pressure on their children to perform well in school because in many cases they are footing the bills. Especially at expensive, private universities where the tuition and room and board bills are extraordinarily high, parents shoulder an enormous financial burden. And they want something for their money. In many respects, parents of students in private colleges have goals similar to legislatures at state-financed universities. They desire and even demand a good return on their capital investment. This is the meaning of the **human capital argument** in education: Education is thought to be a worthwhile investment in a young person, providing, of course, the investment yields a good return. For many parents of students in private universities, this means that their offspring will choose a major that will assure a lucrative job at graduation, will enroll in courses that look good on a résumé, and will get good grades. Some parents who really want to see their money work for them hope their offspring will join the best Greek living unit and select the right kind of spouse.

I have talked to many students who realize the enormous price they must pay in performance pressure in order to have their parents pick up most of the tab for their college education. They are uncomfortably aware that they are no longer children but are an expensive investment, that for them to yield the kind of dividends their parents expect, they must indeed measure up in many ways. There is only the smallest margin for mediocrity or failure.

The human capital model of education was given credibility by former U.S. Secretary of Education William Bennett, a vocal critic of the quality of education in today's universities. Pondering the possibility of his then ten-month-old son someday asking for $10,000 to invest in his own business rather than saving it for a Harvard University education, Secretary Bennett concluded that the business investment might be the superior one.[21]

Getting Grades, Revisited

Based on my years of experience and on the research literature in this area, I believe that the most significant identity peg for students while on campus is their GPA. When all is said and done, and despite all the rhetoric about "learning for its own sake," the ultimate measure of a student's success while in college is the average of the grades received. Grades often determine students' choice of major, whether they can pledge a fraternity of sorority, membership in honor groups and organizations, admission into postgraduate education, and qualification for fellowships. There is nothing quite as efficient and ostensibly fair as a GPA requirement to keep some students out and let others in when the university feels it needs to be selective about something. Nor is there anything as powerful as grade pressure to prod students into meeting a professor's expectations and demands.

The paradox here, of course, is that though the university pays lip service to the ideals of learning for its own sake, of the glories of knowledge and its pursuit, of love of ideas, students' success in college has little if anything to do with such lofty concepts. It makes little difference whether students accept the ideals or not, as long as their GPA is their entitlement to the privileges and rewards that they have been socialized to seek. The embarrassing moments for college professors occur when students remind us of how hypocritical we are in this regard and just how nearly impossible it is to reconcile the ideal of "knowledge for its own sake" with the demands of a grade point system.

It has been my experience, though, that college students don't really mind the grading system that so completely envelopes their college experience. Since they have been socialized to see their college education as a capital investment, they realize the payoffs must be calculated in measurable ways. Students want to be evaluated because their future success depends on it. My impression is that however pressured students feel about grades and GPAs, they can't imagine any better way of staking claim to future rewards. Unfortunately, under current conditions, apparently the faculty can't either.

An extension of the significance of GPAs for college students is the increasing importance being placed on Graduate Record Exams (GREs), Medical Colleges Admissions Tests (MCATs), Law School Admissions Tests (LSATs), and similar standardized exams that college students must take to gain admission to graduate school.

Here again the ETS fills its gatekeeping function as they help to select our future doctors, lawyers, and professors. College seniors, who have already endured the four years of highly competitive grade-grubbing necessary to sustain a high average, now discover that their performance on a single standardized exam may determine the possibility of a professional career. Many students must experience a sort of "ETS déjà vu," reliving the trepidations and fears of four years earlier when they took the SAT in order to get into the right college in the first place.

And, like four years earlier, they find they can get all kinds of help to prove themselves on GREs, LSATs, and MCATs. At my university, where the lust for professional careers is especially acute, the hallway bulletin boards are covered with advertisements for Kaplan courses and for the Graduate Admissions Preparation Service. For a healthy fee, these organizations will help prepare students for the exams so crucial now in their lives. The Graduate Admissions Preparation Service is notably adept in its use of scare tactics to urge students to sign up. On one slick, colorful advertisement we read: "A single exam score may be more important than your hard-earned G.P.A." And what about this for pressure: "Competition is fierce at the nation's best business schools. Harvard, for example, only has room for about 600 out of the many thousands of high G.P.A. applicants. This may be your most important business decision: Are you willing to make a low-cost high-yield investment in your future?"

Even some professors get in the act by offering short courses in preparing for standardized graduate exams, and there are plenty of student takers. At most universities, mine included, this is serious business indeed, as the university measures its own success by the number of its seniors accepted into law school, medical school, or prestigious graduate business programs. When the numbers are favorable, they are circulated to the admissions office to lure prospective high school seniors. The whole process takes the form of a neat little cycle in which universities try to measure up to each other by touting the success of their graduates and the selectivity of their admissions process. All of this occurs at the expense, both financial and emotional, of the students, whose high GPAs and records of acceptance to professional schools are vitally necessary not only to their own careers and prestige but to the university's as well. Of course, none of this competitive cycle would be possible without the blessing and full cooperation of the faculty—who are only too willing to bestow it.

Anorexia: The Problem Returns

I feel it is important to make one more brief diversion into the special problems of female students. The competitive pressure for grades on university campuses is felt as much by young women as by young men, especially as more women seek careers in business, law, and medicine. In fact, for women to succeed in these fields, they must often outperform men to gain recognition and opportunities. College women, then, are very grade conscious.

Aside from measuring up in grades, though, college women still must measure up as females, and though the pressure to earn a "Mrs. degree" is pretty much a thing of the past (at least most of my women students say it is), there remains the pressure to be popular, to be datable, to have "good looks," and, on some campuses, to conform to the standards of beauty and femininity set by sororities.

Given this situation, college women find the university milieu an extension of the high school environment, where looks count as much as brains and women are pressured to conform to feminine stereotypes of dress and beauty. The preoccupation with thinness carries over into the university setting, where we see women students jogging, enrolling in exercise spas, dieting, and reading popular women's magazines for the latest figure ideals.

As we might expect under these conditions, eating disorders among college women have become a significant problem. At the university where I teach, a small liberal arts institution in the Midwest, a therapist who specializes in eating disorders is now on campus once a week, seeing students. In 1995–1996 she logged 199 hours counseling students, mostly women, who had eating disorders or who had important problems with body image.

During a campus convocation at the start of the 1996 school year, this counselor told her largely female audience that many college women have trouble with body images. Too many women, she admitted, were trying to emulate *Cosmopolitan* magazine's models, counting calories and grams of fat and exercising relentlessly to stay thin. She told her audience that modern women have the traditional mandate to be "people pleasers," especially to please men. Yet as moderns, women are urged to be competitive in the world as well. Women want to gain power, and power over their bodies is one way of coping; dieting and compulsive exercise are among the ways women try to control their bodies. Her advice to college women? Throw away the scales!

Through the eyes of an experienced counselor we can see that even though women in college are often under the severe strain of having to measure up academically in ways that will assure them slots in professional schools or in corporate life upon graduation, they must do this in a manner that affirms their femininity and physical attractiveness, proving that as women they have the right stuff, being able to do well yet look good. The often contradictory nature of these demands (for time devoted to looking good is time lost to studying) takes its toll, in the form of eating disorders, depression, and other forms of self-destruction, on too many women.

The Résumé Builder

Recently, in a course that I was teaching, the class discussion for the day centered on modern alienation, and somehow the focus narrowed to the college campus and the fact that students often join organizations in order to find social support. One young woman, Lydia, shed a different light on the subject when she told us that she knew of several students at the university, especially seniors, who joined certain organizations in order to add things to their résumé. When I expressed some surprise at this, Lydia took it in stride: "Well, you know what we students have become? We're résumé builders. That's what counts now."

As is so often the case in these matters, students have a way of knowing themselves better than anyone gives them credit for. Isn't this precisely what we have been hearing about for several years—the growing careerism among college students and the corresponding lack of social and political idealism? There is some truth to this, though I hope to show a bit later that the picture is a lot more complex.

But students engage in **résumé building**—choosing activities and associations because they look good on a résumé—because they are under tremendous pressure to make their education pay off. What better way to assess how well one has done in college than to be admitted to postgraduate professional school or to land a good job? The measured self among college students means proving to oneself, to parents, and to peers that one has performed well and succeeded by signing one's first contract. To that end, most colleges today are committing substantial resources to their career centers. Students receive help in making career decisions, handling employer interviews, and writing résumés and cover letters.

I'm always amused but somewhat chagrined to see senior males, who otherwise would never wear anything but shorts, jeans, T-shirts, baseball caps, and sneakers, show up for their employment interviews in three-piece suits, polished dress shoes, dark socks, fresh haircuts, and shaves. They are the picture of politeness and studied formality.

Of course, they know what counts most at that stage of their college experience. During the senior year, the joys of extended adolescence in college are nearly over, and the sobering reality of sending résumés, interviewing, and finding a good job has just begun.

Looking good on paper can be just as important as personal appearance in landing a job; thus, students learn to load their résumés. If my student Lydia is correct, this means joining organizations one cares little about to have a few more impressive items on the résumé than the next person does. Also, for some students this means avoiding certain situations and activities for fear of having them reflect negatively on a record. Students may refrain from getting involved in campus activism because an arrest might spoil their official record. More likely, student activism has little appeal to most students because it is hardly something employers look for on a résumé. Political protest is not what is defined as campus leadership at the career center.

Résumé building, then, emerges out of practical student concerns raised by career and placement centers and their officials. To get jobs, to measure up as a prospect, men and women must perform well in interviews, which means they must sell themselves. They must appear to be the kind of person an employer is looking for, even though they may not be. Campus interviews are exercises in impression management, the presentation not of an authentic and genuine personality or of personal values but of an acceptable self, a self that has been measured countless times and that in a variety of ways has proven worthy of approval.

Résumés are not much about who the student really is—only about the person he or she can pretend to be. Even summer and part-time jobs are faked by being upgraded and retitled to make them sound more responsible and sophisticated than they really are. A clerk in a drugstore becomes a member of the sales staff; a camp counselor is retitled a "recreation consultant."

Résumés can become dossiers in which students keep track of themselves. They provide their own surveillance now, and there is little need for the Student Affairs Office to play Big Brother to the students, a situation so feared and despised by students in the 1960s. Each student in the quest for a lucrative career or admission into professional school conducts his or her own oversight in the quest for an attractive placement file and impressive résumé. In order to secure the kind of file employers seek, each student will police him- or herself, avoiding the morally sticky situations and embracing those with good résumé potential.

That students should become résumé builders is not surprising, though I was startled to hear my student put it so baldly. Concern with one's résumé is rooted in the students' fear that their educations will not pay off, that the return on investment will be meager. Students are not very well informed about political and international events, but they know enough about the shape and direction of the U.S. economy to be as pessimistic about it as many corporate leaders and economists. Though there will be opportunities for young people, competition will be stiff, and victory will go to those who measure up best.

Many companies anticipate significant cutbacks in the number of college graduates they will hire. Moreover, the higher salaries associated with the fewer jobs will go to the applicants with the highest grades and best internships. And increasing numbers of college graduates will be tested for drug use and AIDS.

This is not a scenario to inspire the hearts of college students. They now find that they must not only measure up in academics and internships but they must also be drug free and unexposed to the AIDS virus. What more will be expected of them as young adults? Is it surprising that, instead of looking to build new civilizations or Great Societies, today's students are concerned mostly with building résumés, placement files, and marketable self-images?

David L. Warren, president of Ohio Wesleyan University, spent the first several months of his new presidency living in the dormitories, getting to know the students there on a more personal level.[22] His impression was that the students were indeed frightened about their future and that they thus tended to insulate themselves through the acquisition of things and possessions. Maybe the truth is that when young people can't be who they really want to be, their need to have things is exaggerated; possessing things substitutes for an authentic life and identity. Readers familiar with the work of Karl Marx will recognize in that statement a very loose paraphrase of one of his central ideas.

Dr. Warren did discover, however, that deep inside college students was an element of idealism and concern for others; but it will not surface unless nurtured. And, I might add here, not only nurtured but rewarded within the context of university life.

Are we then indeed raising generations of young people whose only sense of accomplishment and self-worth is derived from those performances that can be measured, quantified, and externally evaluated? Will our measurement mania drive young people so firmly into the measured self that there will be little opportunity for them to establish identities and personhoods that are in any way genuine? David Elkind once described American adolescents as "all grown up" with "no place to go."[23] In a society fueled by the performance ethic, we might just as accurately identify them as "all measured up with no room to be." With so much of their lives measured and directed toward successful performance, can young people find any meaning or value in their existence apart from living up to someone else's expectations?

I'm aware that some critics of my argument might remind us that these pressures are much worse in Japan; evidence is abundant that the Japanese are even more performance oriented and competitive than we are. Doesn't the Japanese culture emphasize competitive extremes that even U.S. capitalists worry about? We also have evidence about Japanese schools, that students there study longer, harder, and in a more competitive environment than do their U.S. counterparts. Aren't the pressures on Japanese youth even more severe, since a poor examination score early in their school career can mark them for a low-level occupational career as an adult?

All of this may be true. It would be difficult to deny it, but I don't think we are led to conclude that we should emulate Japan just because their competition is more extreme than ours. I will have much more to say about this issue in the concluding chapter of this book, when we look more closely at the implications of competition for economic well-being and human life.

For now, though, and with respect to young people in the United States, I think it is hardly any kind of a balm for them to know that Japanese students and teenagers have it worse than they do. We certainly don't apply this rationale when it concerns our physical health and well-being. If it could be shown that the rate of lung cancer among Japanese is twice as high as among Americans, would we then consider lung cancer no longer a problem or reduce our efforts to find a cure for it? I hope that we wouldn't. Knowing that the suicide rate among Japanese youth is greater than among U.S. young people, which it is, should not make us rest any easier or deter us from seeking ways to reduce the competitive pressures that our own adolescents are facing. We must do this for the sake of our young people as human beings and for the sake of our society's future since measurement mania has yet to establish itself as the best and only motivator of human effort and accomplishment.

I think we can conclude this chapter by arguing that as a society it would be greatly beneficial to define just what it is that we want young people to accomplish, and what we hope or want for them as our future. Their voices should be heard too, as they speak about the kind of selves and identities they feel comfortable in. What if the conclusions drawn from dialogue reveal a desire for maturity in leadership, generosity and caring as future parents, sensitivity, wisdom, and honest productivity as workers, neighbors, and fellow citizens in a democratic, pluralistic society? Could it in any way be established that the best way to lead young people to these shared ideals is through constant measurement, unremitting testing and evaluation, competitive frenzy, quantitative and scientific "achievement" norms, and the encouragement of adherence to gender stereotypes? I don't think so.

As we will see in Chapter 4, adults in the United States are driven by the same competitive pressure and measurement mania as are adolescents. Adulthood in the performance era is hardly more humane, effective, or accomplished. New values and premises for human action must be promulgated if children, adolescents, and adults are to be free from the constraints of the measured self.

Key Terms

1. Reference Group
2. Impression Management
3. Peer Group
4. Generalized Other
5. Peer Paralysis
6. Commodified Identity
7. Labeling Process
8. Anomie
9. Human Capital Argument
10. Résumé Building

Review Questions

1. What are reference groups and is it important to identify them?
2. Explain Goffman's concept of a managed impression. How is this linked to identity?
3. How do peer groups contribute to a person's sense of self? In what ways do adolescent peer groups contribute to the rigid conformity among adolescents?

4. What are some of the ways that adolescents are pressured to have a commodified identity?
5. What is the major shaper of identity among adolescent women?
6. Why is academic achievement so important in defining selfhood among middle-class adolescents? In what way is academic achievement a source of stress?
7. How does organized athletic competition contribute to the measured self among adolescents?
8. How can undue concern with body image lead to eating disorders among female adolescents?
9. What is the feminist perspective on adolescent eating disorders?
10. How does the concept of the generalized other help us understand the power of social control among adolescents?

Discussion Questions

1. How do you achieve compromise in the following areas between your personal standards and the expectations of others?

    A. Academic achievement
    B. Body image (looks)
    C. Athletic competition
    D. Career goals

2. Describe some of the peer groups at the high school you attended. What were the criteria (informal) for membership into these peer groups? What happened to those who were excluded?
3. Is there too much grade pressure in college today? How do you cope with it? Are there other, better ways to evaluate academic performance than by grades? How are grades a form of social control?
4. How common are eating disorders among college women in your living unit or on your campus? Are college men also having to conform to a body image?
5. From which of the following sources do you feel the most pressure to be academically successful?

    A. Self
    B. Parents
    C. Peers
    D. Anonymous "others" (for example, future employment potential)

6. How do your fellow college students build their résumés on your campus? Do you know of any students who choose activities solely on the basis of résumé potential?
7. Describe some sources of stress for modern adolescents different from the ones described in this chapter (academics, body image, athletics). Which of these have been stressful for you personally?

Activities

1. Interview one of the counselors in the Student Affairs office of your college or university. Ask what is being done on campus to help women cope with body image issues and the prevention and treatment of eating disorders. Report your findings to the class.
2. Investigate how some high schools and colleges are trying to reduce academic competition at their schools. What alternatives are they developing with respect to evaluating student performance? You might start by browsing through education periodicals or asking someone in the education department at your university.
3. Select a sample of teen-oriented magazines and conduct a mini-content analysis of the themes in the magazine. What are some of the ways that they portray "successful" adolescent life? What sorts of messages are being sent to adolescents in the product advertisements?

4

The Measured Self in
the Middle Years

Before we look at some of the performance dilemmas faced by men and women in midlife, we need to introduce the important sociological concepts relevant to this discussion. I want to frame the analysis of the measured self in midlife within an understanding of gender roles and status achievement. For I think that the pressures to measure up for middle-aged Americans go to the very core of how these persons see themselves as men and women.

In sociology we make an important distinction between sex and gender. Sex is considered a biological phenomenon; it refers to the physical characteristics that distinguish males from females. **Gender** is the socially and culturally determined set of traits and behaviors that are expected of men and women in a society.[1]

Sociologically, gender categories are held to be socially constructed categories of behavior. That is, in society males are socialized to be "masculine" and females are socialized to be "feminine." Masculinity and femininity are social constructs in that there is variability among different cultures as to what constitute masculinity and femininity. For instance, in some cultures aggressive behavior is associated primarily with masculinity; however, in other cultures aggressive behavior might be appropriate for both males and females.

Through socialization we learn what is expected of us as females or males. Throughout our lives, and I argue especially in midlife, our feelings, thoughts, and actions, indeed our very sense of who we are, often reflects the cultural definitions of gender. Are we measuring up to what society expects of men and women in these years of our lives?

Often these social roles are **gender stereotypes,** that is, mental images of what we typically associate with one gender or the other. When we associate passivity, dependence, and emotion with feminine gender roles and aggression, independence, and unemotionality with masculine gender roles, we are stereotyping these roles. For we know that they may or may not be perfectly correlated with how men and women act in our society. Nevertheless, in the process of gender socialization that takes place in the home, school, and media, certain gender traits are extolled as being the preferred or expected traits associated with males and females.

Finally, a word about stratification (and we will have more to say about this concept in Chapter 5). By social stratification, sociologists refer to the different types of reward in society that people can receive: wealth, power, and prestige.[2] Max Weber, whose theories of rationality we looked at in Chapter 1, once referred to the unequal distribution of esteem or prestige as a **status system.** Prestige is subjective, that is, it cannot be easily measured or counted, and it is related to how others view us. Status is often connected with wealth and income, for though money cannot purchase prestige, in our society status "symbols," such as cars, clothing, club memberships, and home furnishings, all contribute to one's status and can be bought. In midlife one's status attainments, the sense of esteem and self-worth that come from "making it" in society, loom very large indeed. Part of the measured self in midlife is the determination of where we rank in the various hierarchies of adult status and privilege.

*   *   *

With the concepts of gender roles and status system in mind, it is time now to look at the performance ethic for adults in midlife.

As do many contemporary periodicals, *New York Magazine* runs a "Strictly Personal" column in which lonely, single, striving adults can reach out to other like-minded persons searching for the ideal lover or mate. Readers of one issue of *New York Magazine* found the following classified advertisement among the many appearing that month:

Inner virtue is what I'm looking for in a female partner—a strong identity, reinforced by solid ethical standards, consistently reflected in the way you lead your life. That is the kind of personal symmetry I respect and can grow to love. You should also be very bright (a graduate degree would be preferable), young (26–34), tall (5'8" or taller), athletic (hopefully work out intensely several times a week and love one or two sports with a passion), healthy, physically affectionate, and very, very attractive in a natural, non-plastic sense. I am an over-educated, financially secure capitalist with his own successful investment company who is very tall, trim, muscular and works out every day. I love to ski, scuba dive, horseback ride, play racquetball, etc. I am told that I'm very attractive (used to model) in a natural way. Please send bio, photo (a must) and phone number. No smokers.[3]

One wonders whether in all of New York City there exists such a woman. And if she does, surely some man has gathered her up in marriage already. Or one might be tempted to guess that any woman who can measure up to all the other criteria demanded by that secure capitalist would probably be a nervous chain-smoker or have already come completely unraveled emotionally.

And lest we imagine that such idolatrous concern with exalted femininity is an obsession that only swinging New York City males succumb to, the following personal advertisement for the unattached that appeared in an issue of *Mother Earth News* should convince us otherwise:

Dynamic, successful, strong, handsome, white Southern Christian, 38, 6'5", Ivy League, Europe education, real estate developer, animal lover, seeks innocent blue-eyed, Christian, country girl, 19–25 for permanent love affair, many children, country life. Ideally very bright, unpretentious, warm, soft, lovable, very feminine; likes animals, books, piano, older men, exploring life's mysteries; not drugs, discos, nightlife, fashion, feminism. Photo.[4]

It is interesting, isn't it, that devotees of *Mother Earth News*, who supposedly have eschewed the excesses of modern technical culture, have become willing participants in it.

Much can be made of these advertisements, but I don't want to run the risk of taking them too seriously. After all, it can be argued that although these men are seeking an "ideal," probably they will or already have settled for something less. Our Southern Christian might find a Jewish woman who otherwise fits his requirements; the secure capitalist might be satisfied with a woman barely five feet tall who has all the other virtues he was looking for.

However, there is something uncomfortable and insidious in these "personals" that seek perfection in a future mate or lover. How many among us can measure up to standards such as these? And who would want to?

Likewise, we might wonder about the kinds of men and women being created in our culture who would hold up such a measuring rod to a prospective mate. Whether these "personals" are intended to be mildly amusing or are simply a puffing-up of expectations, they do point disconcertingly to the dehumanizing effect of the performance ethic in our culture. For these advertisements, as silly and unrealistic as they appear to be, show us how far the performance culture has come in reinforcing the measured self.

The adult years in the United States offer little refuge from the relentless pressures to measure and assess identity according to prevailing cultural standards of gender, attractiveness, success, and so on. There is no haven or period of life where such pressures disappear completely, though perhaps in the adult years they assume a special force, intensity, and uncomfortable quality. The measured self in the adult years is often accompanied by a heightened sense of urgency not felt by children and adolescents. For the younger a person is in our culture, the more life chances he or she sees ahead. Failures to meet performance standards can be addressed and corrected by further schooling, self-improvement courses, orthodontia, popular literature, television, and so on. And young people have relatively more freedom and time to develop an acceptable self and lifestyle. Their lives yet lie before them, as they learned from various commencement speeches along the way.

Adults in our society have a much more circumscribed grace period; failures to measure up are not as easily forgotten or dismissed. Though corrections for performance failure can be taken, there is an increased sense of immediacy. Not only can failures in adult measurement standards have quick and dramatic results, but there are far fewer years left to make adjustments and accommodations.

Career success, finding the ideal mate or lover, and living up to gender expectations are all performance standards that tend to converge rapidly and forcefully in midlife. Adults must successfully navigate these waters in the time span available to them. Their future is now. Youth's postponed dreams, dreams of money, success, the perfect mate, and the best of children, must be realized now; for if not now, then when? Old age awaits, and in U.S. society those who haven't made it by fifty are not likely to make it at all. Moreover, whatever one's youthful measurement failures, the adult years offer a time of life to make up for them, to measure up and to perform as one had all along hoped to. It is in the adult years that the performance culture offers the greatest, most unrestricted opportunities and rewards for those who succeed. But it is also in the adult years that failure to meet standards is least tolerated and most feared.

Reading the personal ads cited earlier, one cannot help but feel these men's sense of urgency, their fear that time is running out in their search for an ideal mate. Having proven themselves successful in business, they must now measure up in everything else, in finding a culturally attractive mate to share their successful lifestyle. And perhaps what these two men dread most is not that they might have to live alone the remainder of their days but that they have already "failed" to find the kind of feminine ideal so valued and extolled in American culture. "Why must I resort to magazine advertisements," they must ask themselves, "when other successful men I know have already found what they sought?" In the adult years, the search for an ideal mate is far more immediate than were teenage fantasies of "someone, someday," and the process of mate selection can become an anxious quest.

However desperate the search for an ideal mate might be, an even more central dilemma for adults in our society is the search for the ideal self. Indeed, the idealized mates of these personals, those we think ideal, are really mirrors of our self-definitions, of what we think we are and what we like about ourselves. But the quest for selfhood in a culture driven by the performance ethic is enacted within the measuring-up process. The self we can acquire lies within the possibilities offered by the culture, and, as I've argued throughout this book, the possibilities of being are limited and constrained by external, consumer-oriented, measured criteria. As David Reisman pointed out in the early 1950s, the United States is now characterized by the dynamic of the **other-directed personality**,[5] that is, a self acquired neither by a commitment to an interior private ideal nor by the values and norms of tradition but in conformity to the most current measures of a successful personality. Who we are is not derived from the wellspring of an inner life but in response to what we think others are like, to what others are doing, or to what we feel others want us to become.

Parallel to the performance culture is the approval society. What we really want and seek ultimately is approval, to be well liked and accepted. And what better way to accomplish this than striving to prove ourselves, to show that we can measure up in all things? And if our mates and lovers are both reflections and stimuli of our self-image, then they too must measure up and be worthy of approval. What our Southern Christian and secure capitalist are seeking is not only someone who validates their own lifestyles and values but someone who can draw approval from society.

The effects of the cultural performance ethic on self-identity are most pronounced among the middle and professional classes of the United States, and it is on their lifestyles, practices, and pressures that I intend to focus in this chapter.

What are the measuring rods for successful middle-class striving? I would argue that they are many and diverse, but I want to collapse a large number of performance arenas into three general domains of middle-class and professional life: Middle-class adults are faced with measuring their life's worth and success with respect to gender ideals (the masculinity/femininity dilemma), parenting (supermom/superdad), and the more traditional and familiar social measurement (status achievement). Few middle-class adults are free from performance demands in these domains, though on an individual level persons may make accommodations or attempt to cleave to a life course emphasizing one domain over another. Not many adults can create an approved lifestyle ignoring the performance pressure in all three of these arenas.

It will be instructive for us to examine in more detail how the performance ethics in these three areas affect the lives of middle-class women and men and the consequences for personal identity, family life, and career.

The Masculinity/Femininity Dilemma

It is becoming increasingly difficult, perhaps impossible, for adults to lead authentically human lives because they are so pressured to measure up to gender stereotypes.

Historian Joe Dubbert shows that current male stereotypes date back to the original Puritan ethic, which posited faith and work as the keys to salvation.[6] However, by the late nineteenth century, work alone had become the dominant goal of American males and the source of their identity. Of equal consequence, the developing ethos of capitalism held that long hours of hard work defined the "ideal man," and if he was too tired for home and family life, so be it. Capitalist values stressed that home and family were to become the province of women, who could there prove their femininity in ordering emotional life and domestic bliss. Moreover, males in the nineteenth century were expected to be intensely interested in athletic competition because male character was thought to be forged in competitive struggles.

A similar line of argument is advanced by historian Peter Stearns in his analysis of gender socialization.[7] Both masculine and feminine imagery tended to solidify in the nineteenth century with emergence of the stereotype of the "middle-class man," a rugged, competitive, sexually aggressive male. As might be expected, female stereotypes coalesced around the opposite ideal: Women were considered sexually passive, emotional, gentle, and noncompetitive. Males were assumed to be the more rational of the two and therefore the more suited for competitive careers outside the home. Women, too emotional to think very clearly, could only muddle through work in the home.

Industrial capitalism exploited the masculine image. Successful businesses were thought to be constructed by the manly traits of competition and aggression, further strengthening the idea that business affairs were essentially a man's undertaking. Business was soon considered to be a battle: Competitors were fought, and economic wars were won and lost.

Stearns contends that many men developed a love/hate relationship with business. Though they felt it was good that men were aggressive, they thought it a shame that they had to be. Eventually, there was a grudging recognition that men had and needed to accommodate an emotional side. However, rather than giving room to their own emotional potential, males sought the needed emotional balance in their relationships with women. The emotional, passive female was necessary to complement the rational, aggressive male. Women were idealized as the guardians of the morality principle, staying at home and displaying the essence of purity and goodness.

The association of masculinity with work and business has continued into the present, though it is now accompanied by the dilemmas that unemployment and loss of property pose for many middle-class men. By the twentieth century, industrial capitalism found it increasingly impossible to guarantee work for all men, and traditional male property rights gave way to large-scale class struggles for property and goods. How could the propertyless and unemployed males measure up to the ideals of masculinity? (This problem will be addressed more specifically with respect to lower-class males in Chapter 5.)

Studies show that middle-aged white males now make up the majority of workers in the U.S. labor force. Their proportion is decreasing, and it is estimated that near the turn of the century middle-aged white males will account for only 39 percent of the labor force.[8]

Moreover, new labor technology, such as computers, reduce the need for much of the human and individual judgment and decision making that once were considered part of the manliness of work. Shoshona Zuboff argues that the intelligent technology of computers substitutes algorithms of decision rules for human judgments.[9] In other words, technical, mechanical information systems are now replacing the human capacities to make judgments and decisions at work.

In the absence of job security, property rights, and manly work, males must achieve prowess through consumerism, especially purchases of automobiles, which have become a symbol of masculinity. The powerful, fast sports car allows men to exercise their maleness by driving aggressively and competitively. Males join in the automobile subculture, drawn to the enticing sexual imagery and themes of automobile advertisements.

Stearns contends that the **corporate man**—the male who measures up to masculine ideals of rationality, aggressiveness, and competitiveness in his climb to the top of the corporate career ladder—emerged in the twentieth century. The corporate man risks failure, however; he faces the possibility of moving down the ladder rather than up. Such a possibility represents more than an uneven career: It is an assault on the male's ability to live up to masculine ideals.

During recent decades, a variety of writers have documented the solidification during the twentieth century of this masculine ideal as the measuring stick for the American male. Writer Andrew Kimbrell contends that one of the modern renditions of masculinity is **male as a machine**—not a real person but a stereotype.[10] Men have become dominated by the performance ethic because competitive performance is thought to be manly. Men can hardly think of themselves in other ways. The American male must prove constantly that he can measure up, but in doing so he becomes the stereotype.

For example, consider again the personal ads quoted earlier. The secure capitalist and the Southern Christian were hardly persons at all. They were, in fact, stereotypes of masculine ideals searching for stereotypes of femininity. Describing themselves as strong, virile, aggressive, physically robust, and secure did not reveal these men as anything other than someone desperately trying to live up to the cultural ideal of masculinity. The proud bearing so unmistakable in these personals is not the assurance of someone who has achieved a degree of self-understanding and insight. Though these two men profess a desire for women who are warm and passionate, there is little in their self-description to indicate that they could reciprocate warmth and passion in any way. In fact, the qualities they seek in a woman are not only stereotypical for women but are the very qualities that atrophied in these men years earlier as they sought to achieve the masculine ideal. Indeed, they have busied themselves in what Marc Fasteau has called the "flight from passion."[11] And having flown from the passionate ethic that could have been theirs, they seek it as an ideal, as a feminine stereotype, though neither man understands it, has experienced it, or desires it as a personal quality. Like men of the nineteenth century, they want a warm, sensitive woman to complement their rational, aggressive personalities. Only in a relationship with a woman who represents the feminine ideal can these men feel completely human.

One gets the impression that these are macho males, even though the 1960s and 1970s were thought to have softened the machismo element in American maleness, substituting a more pliant, gentle, and sensitive masculine ideal. Whether or not the macho man standard ever disappeared, or even temporarily abated, for middle-class males, the 1980s ushered in a period when the macho stereotype found renewed favor, support, and recognition. Once again it was acceptable for men to act like real men and flex their muscles a little. Consider the box-office successes in the 1980s and 1990s: stars such as Sylvester Stallone, Tom Cruise, and Clint Eastwood. Rambo dolls and other models of muscular fighting figures can be found in stores throughout the country. Clint Eastwood traded on his tough-guy image briefly to launch a successful political career in California.

Similarly, the jingoistic political style of President Ronald Reagan and his often bellicose foreign policy reinvigorated the macho ideal in politics, where real men as heads-of-state won't be pushed around. Reagan's popularity in office, particularly among men, was due in part to his revival of the sagging masculine ideal and his willingness to assume "tough" stances on issues. Even President Bill Clinton feels the need to be a masculine president, and he fulfills that need through aggressive policies toward Iraq.

Though middle-class and professional men don't necessarily aspire to the Rambo or Dirty Harry ideal, they secretly admire their successes and approach. And though middle-class males might not have the physique of a Stallone, they seek the next best thing in physical fitness. Andrew Kimbrell refers to the ideal male physique as the "techno-body"—muscular, fit, and lean[12]—and in pursuit of this physique men buy "muscle machines," whose annual sales have now reached 750 million dollars.

For modern males life can be thought of as a quest to measure up to the masculine ideals associated with competitive success, physical and sexual aggressiveness, rationality, and coolness under fire. The problem for many middle-class males comes at midlife in the area of occupational and career success, when they ask "How well have I done?"

Males during midlife do a lot of stocktaking, evaluating their careers and professional accomplishments. Many males experience a decline in midlife, finding the competitive struggle difficult to maintain. Crisis often ensues, precipitated by changes in lifestyles, values, and societal expectations.

Feelings of self-respect become a major concern for men in midlife, and their feelings of self-respect are linked to their assessments of how well they measure up as men to what is expected of them. Living up to the masculine ideal and performing well contributes most to their feelings of self-worth.

Current trends in the economy will have direct bearing on many men's ability to be positive about their career opportunities. As increasing numbers of women enter the contemporary job market and compete on more or less equal footing for scarce economic and career rewards, the opportunities for men to measure up and successfully fulfill the traditional masculine role will shrink. How many men at midlife will face the reality of contracting expectations and possibilities as competition between genders becomes more intense? And what will it mean to the self-respect of men in their forties when they lose promotions and career opportunities to the women they were socialized to believe couldn't be very competitive or aggressive?

One interesting area in which the competitive struggle between the sexes is being carried out is personal attractiveness. Steven Florio, the publisher of *Gentleman's Quarterly*, acknowledged that in the new economic competition between men and women, personal appearance can be used to acquire an edge. Florio comments: "Our men may want to look good for its own sake. But a large percentage of them are also competing with women for jobs, and they know looks count."[13] Thus, *Gentleman's Quarterly* readily offers its readers scores of advertisements for personal products to make men look good enough to measure up successfully against women. Here, then, is a further extension of the commodified identity and measured self, a self that is not necessarily authentic or real but exists in appearances only.

For adult women, the performance ethic manifests itself in the feminine stereotypes or ideals that women are supposed to pursue or measure themselves against. Whereas the nineteenth-century masculine ideal emphasized competitiveness, rationality, and aggressiveness, the feminine stereotype required passivity, emotionality, and quietude.

Women, especially those of the middle and upper classes, were considered too emotional and passive for the real world of work; their place was in the home, peacefully tending to household chores and taking care of the children.

These images (which even in the nineteenth century did not always square well with reality) carry over into the twentieth century, with some modifications. Although since World War II increasing numbers of women have entered the workforce, the feminine ideal remains: Women fulfill gender expectations by success in mothering and by being a good wife. As Nancy Chodorow (among other writers) points out, women's childcare responsibilities tie them primarily to the private or family orbit of life—the feminine sphere—whereas men's primary sphere is public.[14]

Probably the one change during the twentieth century to the feminine ideal was the emphasis on feminine beauty. The middle-class woman's self is measured and valued with respect to attractiveness of face, hair, and figure. As we saw in Chapter 3, women are socialized into the standards of feminine beauty as early as the preteen years. Women are taught to be obsessively concerned with their looks because their personal attractiveness is held up as the key to popularity, mate selection, and, later, career advancement and economic success.

Looking into the mirror becomes second nature for women, many of whom are taught from a young age that a girl never leaves the house without "putting on her face," that cosmetics are a girl's best friend, and that next to a winning personality, nothing gets attention better than good looks. While boys are learning the competitive ethic and getting dirty on the football field, girls are also being steeped in the beauty ethic at home, working on their posture, and learning how to wear the right clothes and how to use makeup. Of course, I'm overgeneralizing here, but my point is to show the early influence of beauty in defining femininity for young women. Women are socialized to see themselves as objects, as symbols of sexual beauty, and to feel best about themselves when they look good enough to have others notice them.

Nowhere do we see the exaltation of feminine beauty more clearly in our culture than in the way feminine appearance is commercialized. Product after product is glamorized and made to look appealing by sexualizing it through the use of female models.

In one of the college courses I teach, my students and I view a remarkable film entitled *Still Killing Us Softly*, which portrays the devastating way Madison Avenue exploits women through advertising. We learn from the film that advertisers can make products seem sexually titillating by using seductive women models in various postures and positions, embracing the product, caressing it. Another tactic advertisers employ that demeans women is the use of glamorous, beautiful models to show off products intended to make a normal, average woman look as attractive as the model. Hair care products, cosmetics, hosiery, undergarments, and so on are modeled by women whose perfection in beauty, it is implied, is the result of using that particular product. As the narrator of *Still Killing Us Softly* reminds her audience, in real life even the models don't look that good. Pictures and films can be doctored to remove blemishes and slight imperfections in complexion or figure. Hours of preparation are necessary to make the model appear perfect.

Popular women's magazines, and there are many of them, could hardly publish a single issue without the cover page featuring a woman with a beautiful face, an unblemished complexion, perfect white teeth, and full-bodied hair. And the reader is encouraged—if she wants to look like the model—to find all the necessary beauty tips, latest diet, and current fashions within that very magazine. If a visitor from another world had only magazine covers to go by in surmising what women looked like, he would never guess that some women have straight, gray hair, moles and freckles, semistraight teeth, and less than ideal figures.

Put succinctly, women's magazines portray a feminine ideal that few women can match. The magazines, by and large, present a distorted reality that women are expected to accept as sane and sensible. Though the fate of most adults is to become gradually bald, gray, overweight, and a little dumpy, the ideals are held out to inspire us to be something we cannot. Few if any women can look like the models in *Vogue*, and trying to measure up to the impossible leaves many women with feelings of inferiority and even self-loathing, thereby damaging their sense of identity, confidence, and well-being. Women are no longer free to age, to dress as they wish, or to maintain figures that aren't sexy or alluring.

With more middle-class women today pursuing careers in business and professional fields, the cult of beauty is now combined with a "today's woman" ideal, emphasizing a feminine toughness, careerism, and success. What many contemporary women's magazines hold up as the feminine standard is the **complete woman,** one who has great looks and figure combined with a successful career and manageable lifestyle. For today's woman, success in beauty or career success alone is not enough; both are now possible and worth striving for.

New Woman is a magazine billed for the "modern woman." Like so many of its genre, it carries the typical features of a contemporary women's magazine, with sections on fashion and beauty, food and decorating, work and money, and, of course, a physical fitness section. (How could a career woman dare be a few pounds overweight?) Sprinkled throughout its pages, *New Woman* contains advice from doctors, psychologists, diet consultants, and other experts, for a woman cannot be expected to make her own decisions. The leitmotif of *New Woman* is that the successful woman today is a juggler and a balancer who never lets her life stray too far in any one direction. A woman should not pursue career success at the expense of her beauty nor be so preoccupied with work that she fails to prepare nutritious meals at home, and she always finds time to stay fit and trim. The modern career woman must measure up in a good many ways, but with plenty of expert advice, product endorsements, and recipe selections, there is no reason she can't perform well. Interestingly, one issue of *New Woman* ran an ad for MENSA seeking new members. To join, all that is needed is an IQ in the ninety-eighth percentile. Have we covered all the bases for our modern woman: beauty, successful career, domestic excellence, good money sense, slim figure, intellectual brilliance? That's not too much to ask, and if this woman is single she will qualify for a date with the secure capitalist, providing she is nearly six feet tall.

Fit as a Fiddle

Among the recent pressures on women, perhaps none is more severe than linking femininity with slimness and fitness. Adolescent females are not alone in facing pressure to keep a slim figure—their youth just makes it a bit easier for them. Women in midlife receive a similar message from husbands, physicians, magazines, and actresses: Real femininity lies in the ability and willingness to stay trim.

We might call this the "Jane Fonda movement," whereby millions of women are trying to diet, exercise, and jog their way to a Fonda-like figure. And Fonda's helpful books on exercise and diet sell by the carload and make her the ultimate winner. She jogs all the way to the bank. Recently, while I was browsing in a Waldenbooks store in a suburban shopping mall, I decided to count the number of diet and exercise books. I found twenty-eight diet books and twenty-five exercise books; not a very scientific survey, but it gave me an idea of the popularity of diets and exercise and of just how far women are now willing to go in their pursuit of physical excellence. With health spas, aerobic dancing classes, diet centers, and "gut busters" and other instruments of torture, is there any good reason for the modern woman not to be trim, flat-tummied, and in great health? Certainly no one can blame Jane Fonda for not doing her part.

Women are the target of a large commercial industry promoting books, exercise tapes and videos, workout programs, running shoes, and so on. Enormous profits are being made by entrepreneurs (Fonda is no exception) playing on women's guilt about their weight or their shape and urging them to conform to the feminine stereotype and measure up as complete women. Slim and trim, bright, beautiful, and driven are now the standards set for the modern middle-class woman who turns to a commercial culture eager to sell her the commodified image that will win approval.

An issue of *Ms.* magazine sheds disturbing and important light on this phenomenon in releasing the results of a reader survey on addiction.[15] Chemical addiction appears to be directly linked to women's search for an ideal self. For example, 64 percent of the women surveyed agreed with the statement "I would like myself better if I were thinner." Of those who answered the survey 34 percent experienced drinking problems, such as blackouts and memory lapses. And the drinkers tended to be women who had experimented with a variety of dieting behaviors. Among the women surveyed by *Ms.* magazine, self-esteem issues were critical in their lives and intersected with issues of food, appearance, and relationships. Perhaps of greater importance, these women were concerned with their image most when their weight was up. In these periods, they became excessively concerned with self.

Women are responding, of course, to the part of the cultural performance ethic that places a great premium on attractiveness. They know what is expected of them. Women also know what happens to other women who fail to measure up. It may come as no surprise, then, that according to the *Ms.* magazine survey, at any given time more than half the U.S. female population is on a diet.

Supermom/Superdad

From the measuring-up pressures associated with gender performance it is but a small step to the second domain of performance anxiety for adults. The terms "supermom" and "superdad" are becoming commonplace, and since much has been written about this issue our analysis will be limited to how the performance ethic played a role in generating the problem.

The phenomenon of parents trying to be supermom and superdad translates essentially into an attempt at "having it all," the attempt to measure up successfully to a variety of (sometimes contradictory) role demands. Having it all defies the traditional argument that division of labor was best for a healthy and happy life at work, in marriage, and in the home. The traditional picture looked like this: Marriage, family, and work roles were divided along gender lines, and men and women were socialized to accept their place and find satisfaction in the division of labor. Upon marriage, the male assumed the role of breadwinner, working outside the home pursuing career success for the good of his family. To be a good father was to work hard and be a good provider. Women who married were expected to remain in the home, taking primary, perhaps full, responsibility for nurturing and socializing children, keeping the home, cooking, cleaning, laundry, and so on.

Scholars tell us that few families in the United States ever really fit this description. It is primarily a middle-class ideal that was reinforced through television shows in the 1950s and 1960s like *Father Knows Best* and *Leave It to Beaver*. But we can understand the supermom/superdad problem today only if we see the traditional gender divisions as a cultural ideal that was accepted as a way of life for several generations of middle-class adults. Though some men helped their wives in the home and assisted with the children and some women worked outside the home, the main source of role fulfillment was found in living up to the traditional expectations of masculinity and femininity. Whether men were successful around the home was only secondary in importance to their success as breadwinners. And though women may have worked outside the home, contributing to the family's income, it was ability as a mother and homemaker that provided the yardstick of her success. If troubles arose in the home, the wife quit work in order to restore domestic order.

Among the middle classes, there is now a blurring of role distinctions and a change in the way success in gender accomplishment is defined. More specifically, being a supermom means that women seek success and accomplishments in all areas—home, marriage, and career. No one role demand claims primary allegiance, and success is expected in all. Superdad is faced with the same expectations.

The prototype of the supermom was Phylicia Rashad, who played Bill Cosby's wife on *The Cosby Show*. Here was a woman who was a successful lawyer, a gracious, consoling, and understanding mother to her children, and an intelligent, open, warm, and supportive wife to her husband. And Cosby, for all his problems as a physician, father, and husband (without the problems of a comic foil there would be no situation comedy), was the perfect superdad—urbane, witty, insightful, successful in the office, at home, and in the bedroom.

There is much in our society that tells middle-class adults that they can have it all: not only popular television shows but also how-to books and magazines with advice and checkpoints to instruct men and women in how to measure up, in how to be all things to all people and do it well. But as supermoms and superdads have found, meeting the demands is often impossible, and failure looms just around the corner. *Ms.* magazine once asked writer Pete Hamill to do an article about the new man who "wants it all."[16] Hamill traveled around the country to find out what it was that men wanted. The men he talked to had higher expectations for themselves than most women he interviewed. Men want a successful career, traditional marriage, wonderful children, and modern independence. For example, here is a young stockbroker's wish list: a supportive wife, with a career if she wants one, who is great in bed, beautiful, with a sense of humor, and faithful. (This sounds vaguely like the secure capitalist's wish list.)

The problem that Pete Hamill found for the modern superdad is in combining career and success with time for children at home. When executives work, on the average, fifty-six hours per week, there is not much time for home life.

Hamill concludes that "having it all" is an image of perfection being fed to young Americans who aren't very sure how they will manage. While it could turn out to be mostly fun as on *The Cosby Show,* for many young men the pressures might be far too great. When the chips are down, success for the modern middle-class male does not always or necessarily include changing diapers and chauffeuring kids to the day care center. Though home and family life are important to these career men, they can hardly aspire to be senior executives and still spend a lot of time with their children. Thus, for these men to be modern, their wives must be traditional, a blend that does not always work in the contemporary United States. Witness the divorce rate of the past fifteen years, when nearly one out of two marriages ended in divorce (though the rate has slowed the last few years).

Supermoms have more difficult ordeals, according to Carol Osborn, a former supermom turned normal.[17] Osborn is the founder of Superwoman's Anonymous, an organization providing support for recovering supermoms. Carol Osborn spent thirty-five years trying to be everything she could be: good mother, wife, boss, role model. Ultimately she became very unhappy and felt miserable about herself.

She came to resent the superwoman watchwords—"coping," "balancing," and "juggling"—and the supermom ideal that all roles can be filled to perfection with proper juggling of commitments and balancing of time and coping with problems. Osborn felt she was coming up short; she was experiencing failure and blaming herself for her inadequacies. She eventually discovered that she didn't even want everything.

As a recovering supermom, Osborn now realizes that the popular media stimulate people's needs to have and be everything. Women are shown role models who can cope and be successful, but more often than not these are ideals few women can live up to. And if they could, they would soon be exhausted, as Osborn herself found out when she tried to manage her successful business, maintain her appeal as an attractive and stimulating wife, and be the complete, all-knowing, always caring mother to her children. Eventually she felt physically and mentally drained.

In creating Superwoman's Anonymous, Osborn discovered she was not alone. Hamill also unearthed some failures in his investigation, as we hear from one of the supermoms he interviewed:

"I tried," a 42-year-old woman told me. An investment banker, she married at 35, had two children before she was 38. "I tried like hell to put everything together and just couldn't manage it. Not because I'm weak, I think I'm a strong person. But there simply aren't enough hours in the day to be all the people I tried to be. The economy was booming, I was making good money. But so was my husband. I felt I was being a lousy mother. I was distracted at work. Something had to give. Sure I could have asked my husband to quit his job and stay home, but I don't think he would have done it. So I quit my job. I can't say I'm happier. I'm healthier. I'm less exhausted. I love the children. Of course, I also know that I tried to do something and failed. I'll have to live with that."[18]

How many women in our society, trying to be supermoms, feel the same kind of guilt expressed by this woman? Probably far too many; is it in any way justified or necessary? Hamill wishes things were different, and his remarks provide a fitting summary here: "I wish the relentless pressure in this country to be famous or powerful would ease up, so that more of us—men and women—could lead more civilized lives." I would add to Hamill's list of societal pressures the need to be perfect or "super" in all roles. Only in today's army is it possible to "be all that you can be," and we should realize that that promise is at best merely an advertising slogan and at worst a pressure few of us can endure.

Status Achievement

The third area of competitive pressure in U.S. society, and perhaps the most traditionally recognized, is that of status and economic achievement. This domain is most directly linked to the myth of the American Dream, the myth that through enough hard work, diligence, and perseverance anyone can "make it" in the United States and that everyone should try. And making it is defined in material and careerist terms—moving up the corporate or organizational ladder and becoming financially secure and prosperous. Americans are socialized to think of the pot at the end of the rainbow almost as if it were real and all the gold in it theirs if they work hard and want it badly enough. Status achievement is the most readily comprehended dimension of the performance ethic because it is so directly measurable: by income, number of promotions, size of home purchased, number of BMWs in the garage, number of country-club memberships. Unlike gender stereotypes or superparent ideals, which are often subjective and vague, status achievement produces tangible, material, countable, and comparable results. In this area of performance, the markers of having made it are apparent to oneself and others.

Historically, married women shared the status achievements of their husbands (they also shared in the failures) through the marital agreement; today, increasing numbers of women are trying to achieve high incomes and career success on their own. For women, fulfilling the American Dream faces the extra stumbling block that the corporate, financial, and commercial worlds (in fact, nearly all well-paying work outside the home) have always been dominated by men. Women who want to make it must be all the more hard working, talented, bright, and persevering.

My wife once attended a workshop on "Image and Communication Skills" sponsored by the Business Woman's Training Institute. The trainer that day was a young, energetic, articulate black woman whose motto was "Fake it 'til you make it." Her message to women who desired career success? One must be very concerned about communication skills and image. To be a powerful communicator, one has to control the signals sent in nonverbal communication. She encouraged women to be aware of their style and image because the style of communication is as important as the content. Thus, career-oriented women are openly encouraged to use images and signals to their best advantage as one way of making it in a male-dominated work world. Authenticity or genuineness in personality is far less important than the ability to create a powerful image through style.

Despite such sage advice for career-oriented women, making it remains difficult. Women are indeed making gains in the world of paid work, but barriers to success are still significant. More women today are working in paid occupations. During the past fifty years, for example, the number of women working outside the home has doubled.[19] Within the next decade, six out of every ten new workers will be women. But though the gap between men's earnings and women's earnings has narrowed in recent years, most of this narrowing is accounted for by decreases in men's wages,[20] and women earn less than men even within the same occupation. In sales, for instance, women only earn 56 percent of male earnings. And in professional occupations, women only earn 72 percent of what men do. With respect to advancement, women face what sociologists call **the glass ceiling,** an unacknowledged barrier that blocks them from rising to the top levels of power.[21] Women hold only 2 percent of the top corporate positions in the United States. And they hold only 6 percent of the seats on corporate boards of directors.

Though many women are entering the competitive fray of status achievement, the fact remains that there is only so much room at the top and the competitive pressures are becoming all the more severe. And though men might know the rules of the game better than women, relatively few men will realize their dreams. They will be forced to reduce their expectations and settle for less. But the performance ethic is so deeply internalized by career-oriented men and women that for many there is no turning back or setting sights lower.

"The New Calvinists" is an expression, coined by Richard Thain, business dean of the University of Chicago, being used to describe young adults pursuing career success in Chicago. Thain was referring to the enormous devotion to work now being shown by the upwardly mobile. "This profound devotion to work is a phenomenon of the last four or five years. It's not just among MBA graduates either, but all the way up to the higher executives. The work week has lengthened for all managerial employees."[22] Long, grueling hours are now the key to success since today's companies no longer reward loyalty and length of service with promotions. "The idea of turning fifty and coasting is dead. There are no free rides,"[23] says John Alexander, a management consultant who advises corporations throughout the United States on performance analysis.

Sixty- to seventy-hour work weeks are becoming the standard in investment banking and managerial consulting. The New Calvinist has little time for sleep, let alone home, marriage, and family commitments. Relationships are relegated to the back burner says Melinda, a bank vice president: "Sometimes I ache for someone special to be close to. But, to be honest, I probably wouldn't have the time.[24]

Not all can hope to achieve the wealth of a Wall Street investment banker, but the obligation remains for millions of other adults to find some measure of success in the economic world. The good life is measured precisely in the way adult men and women make something of themselves and surround themselves with the trappings of success. Economic and work life are becoming less valued as ends in themselves; the satisfaction of creating, building, serving, and producing are less important than what one earns and amasses and how quickly one is rising. The measured self in this regard means the self whose occupational life is evaluated not by the strength of internal commitments and satisfactions but by how one's achievements compare to others' achievements, by the questions "To what degree do my accomplishments pale when compared to others', and how are others' achievements diminished relative to mine?"

Perhaps nowhere does this comparison phenomenon, so vital to the measured self, manifest itself as directly as in high school reunions. What better opportunity or occasion to assess how far one has climbed, to compare oneself with others who started from the same point?

In 1992, the editors of *Psychology Today* magazine asked a number of people who had attended their high school reunions to share their experiences.[25] Why did they go, they were asked, and what was it like? For nearly all the men and women interviewed, there was an element of fear and loathing. One woman, a fifty-one-year-old advertising executive, was astonished at the accomplishments of other women, not necessarily intimidated but obviously impressed with how well her female classmates had made out: "We had surprised ourselves. We had become something, tasted success."[26] Yet another woman felt trepidation at attending her reunion because her level of success did not match her youthful aspirations. This forty-year-old insurance claims adjuster admitted: "A half hour before leaving I had a final crisis of confidence. The only single non-mother in my class, I was not leading the impressive life I had planned in 1971. And I wasn't up to repeated interrogations about it."[27]

One man in midlife who attended several reunions found that both success and failure tended to be isolating experiences. A real estate developer at age thirty-eight, this man had experienced the highs and lows of his career. "When I attended my 15th year reunion, I won a Flying Wing award for the person whom least was expected of and who did the best. Perhaps it all went to my head since five years later, having been the first millionaire, I was also the first to go bankrupt." His experiences, however, were similar at both reunions. He felt isolated from his friends at his first reunion when he was highly successful and equally isolated five years later after his career had crashed: "I think everybody thought they would catch what I caught—failure as a highly communicable disease."[28]

But not all those in midlife in our society need a class reunion to remind them of where they stand. Their lot is to constantly compare and appraise themselves in relation to others. All the men and women trying to make it in the years they have remaining before they grow too old or the hour too late know how far they have come and how far they have yet to go. Time presses in on their lives. The demands of the performance ethic require one more pay raise, another notch or two up the corporate ladder, and maybe the building of one last dream home. For these are the only criteria that will satisfy the measured self. And though living up to gender ideals and trying to be a supermom or superdad is important, in the final analysis it is still money and career success that gives meaning to life in the middle years. And though many women today are feeling pressured to have successful careers, it is still primarily middle-aged men whose sense of self is measured by how much they earn and the size of the home to which he brings his bacon. It is these men in their often desperate middle years of achievement to whom Linda, the wife of Willy Loman in Arthur Miller's *Death of a Salesman,* refers when she begs that "attention must be paid to such a person."

Excursus on Sexuality

The performance ethic has permeated sexual relationships among many middle-class adults, adding yet another arena in which men and woman feel constrained and obligated to prove themselves.

Ideally, sexual ecstasy lies in self-abandonment as an escape from the tensions produced in a highly competitive, performance-oriented life. However, in many respects sexuality has become just another competitive arena in which the performance ethic dominates. In place of the intimacy of personal fulfillment in a unique relationship with another person, the measurement ethic in sexuality produces questions like: "Do I get enough?" "Was it good?" "Am I good as a sexual partner?" And, by not so far a stretch, "Am I good enough as a man or woman, hence as a human being?"

Sexuality today has taken on a new dimension of technique, achievement, and mastery. Since the time of Sigmund Freud, it has been believed that repression of sexual desire is the basis of neurosis. The sexual revolution, which began in the 1960s under the impetus of the birth control pill, taught that greater emotional health would result from more and better sex. A central tenet of the counterculture ethos was that sexual frustration was a prime cause of aggressive and antisocial behavior: The slogan "Make love, not war" was not only a popular catchword among those opposed to the Vietnam War; it also reflected a belief that sexual liberation would lead to a less "uptight," more loving world, and even to the end of war.

But as the increasing sense of meaninglessness and anxiety associated with the "me decade" of the 1970s and the selfishness and materialism of the "yuppies" of the 1980s and 1990s has shown, sexual liberation has not reformed the world. Denizens of singles bars and others, married and unmarried, who jumped into the waterbed of polymorphous, pluralistic sex have begun to report ennui, dissatisfaction, and boredom. Quantity, variety, and technique, no matter how exciting they might seem, don't bring the satisfactions they had promised. Quantity and variety don't lead to quality. Mastering the techniques of multiple orgasms, simultaneity, and the other criteria set forth by countless manuals and self-help books to measure how well we're doing in bed doesn't lead to fulfillment.

Such information is good and has undoubtedly helped many people achieve greater sexual fulfillment. On the other hand, the availability of information on sexual behavior has led to the establishment of norms of sexuality, to standards of comparison. People readily measure themselves, and many become dissatisfied.

Performance Anxiety

Joan Liebman-Smith, writing in *Ms.* magazine on a study of adult sexuality, found that many married couples felt pressured into having sex as frequently as the national studies suggested was the norm.[29] A number of couples in her study felt bad when their own frequency of intercourse fell below national norms, as if in some way they were abnormal or inadequate.

Sex counselors and therapists speak of **sexual performance anxiety**—that is, feelings of sexual inadequacy—as a source of psychological problems. One of the major reasons many people seek sexual counseling is that they do not have a desire for frequent sex and feel abnormal about it. In recent years, not "wanting it" often enough has been defined as deviant; lack of sexual desire is often associated with psychopathology.

In addition to sexual desire and frequency of intercourse as measures of healthy sexual performance, orgasm has become a sexual mandate. One of the outcomes of the sexual revolution and the subsequent outpouring of books and studies on sexuality in adults has been the "orgasmic imperative," the idea that men and women must experience orgasm, preferably more than once and simultaneously. Sex therapists report that women experience strong pressures to define their womanhood and femininity with respect to the type and frequency of their orgasms.

Andrew Kimbrell has argued that sexuality for men is bound up with a power image.[30] "Penis power" refers to the male's ability to obtain and maintain an erection. Male sexual power obligates him to subdue his partner and exhaust her! What the contemporary man fears most is impotency, the failure to achieve an erection and to maintain the male power image. Impotency is now considered a modern male health care problem, and the number of impotency clinics is increasing.

The performance ethic in sexuality means that feelings are secondary; what counts most is being able to achieve measurable goals such as multiple and simultaneous orgasms. As both men and women become preoccupied with sexual technique, impotency often results. The more people try to live up to sexual norms, the less they are able to do so, the less enjoyable and pleasurable is sexuality, and the less room there is in sex for love, emotion, and tenderness. For many adults in our society, whose lives are already an endless string of performance appraisals, sexual bliss and abandonment is no longer an alternative to performance pressure but an extension of it.

Sexual Anomie: Expectations Run Wild

The main ideology underlying the sexual revolution, besides the Freudian notion that sexual repression leads to neurosis, is the dogma that Puritanical attitudes toward sex involved widespread hypocrisy, double standards, and unhealthy frustration of natural functioning. At the same time, however, magazines such as *Playboy* made "girly" pictures respectable to the middle class by presenting them in a glossy context intermingled with serious fiction, articles on public issues, and so on. The modern male, single or married, was for virtually the first time able to have an excuse for looking at pictures of nude women: "There are many good articles" became the screen, so to speak, behind which sexually "sophisticated" men could avoid the shame and stigma that had previously been attached to indulging in sex-oriented magazines and French postcards.

Such magazines, however, also had the unfortunate effect of raising the sexual expectations of many men. The man looking at the photos of young women in *Playboy* and similar magazines and reading the descriptions of extensive, often esoteric sexual delights in the "Playboy Advisor" columns inevitably compares his own sexual experience and the characteristics of his sexual partners with the very high standards of beauty, performance, and variety set before him in naked glory and tantalizing words. With few exceptions, the reader would find his own sex life and sexual partner lacking to some, perhaps a great, degree. Men could respond by trying to find partners to match or come close to the models in the magazines, and in fact many have done this. This means, however, that women are forced to try to conform to a very narrow range of body type, appearance, and other measured characteristics, which leads to dieting mania, anorexia, constant concern over appearance, and other negative consequences.

Similarly, contemporary magazines catering to modern, liberated women, featuring centerfolds of macho men and male athletes, create measuring-up pressures on men to develop the kinds of muscles, mustaches, and body builds necessary to be attractive. Hence, any man who wants to be sexy, appealing, and worth having had better spend plenty of time in the gym or health spa.

For married men and women, the sexual norms and body builds featured in *Playboy* and *Playgirl* magazines, though providing enjoyable bases for daydreams, also undermine their tendencies to be satisfied with their mates. The performance ethic can create the kind of sexual ideal that few can live up to, though many may try. Marital discord and frustration often follow when both partners try to measure up to impossible sexual imagery and demands and as couples confuse what is real and important in their marriages with what is fantasy and probably irrelevant.

And so we have come nearly full circle now: The performance pressures that began in childhood continue into the adult years. From cradle to computer camp, from Little League to Junior League, from boardroom to bedroom, we relentlessly pursue the measured self, seeking approval and measuring our lives against quantitative standards, impossible ideals, and current stereotypes. Our culture promises individuality and personal freedom but demands mostly a tight conformity and delivers an identity gained through commodities and media images that can never really be ours. Though on the surface we appear to be in control of our lives and destinies, we are actually driven by performance imperatives that demand that we be and have what is faddish, unhealthy, impossible, and often irrelevant to real human needs and desires. Thus, we live the half-life partly for ourselves but mostly for others, and not always for the others who really count and care for us. We live for mysterious and generalized others hidden behind commercial images, media stereotypes, and capitalist economic and educational requirements. Much of our interior life, of our inner needs and desires, is sacrificed in order to meet externally imposed standards that compel us without our knowing it. These are the perils, often unrecognized, of unconscious social forces that limit freedom and human uniqueness.

So far I've talked exclusively about how the performance ethic affects the lives and identities of the middle and professional classes. It remains now to assess the impact of the performance ethic on working-class Americans and on the poor and minorities. For they too face measuring-up pressures, particularly economic ones, as they attempt to make a living, raise their families, and have a life in a highly competitive, credential-oriented economic system. As we shall see, their economic fate and chances to live a humane life lie in their ability to measure up and compete for scarce resources in an era that demands more and more in the way of diplomas, degrees, and credentials if one is to make a living. What is the destiny of the poor and the working-class in an economic system that expects so much?

Key Terms

1. Gender
2. Gender Stereotypes
3. Status System
4. Other-Directed Personality

5. The Corporate Man
6. Male as a Machine
7. The Complete Woman
8. The Glass Ceiling
9. Sexual Performance Anxiety

Review Questions

1. How do sociologists distinguish between sex and gender?
2. In what way are gender categories socially constructed?
3. Give an example of a gender-role stereotype.
4. Why is status attainment so important for persons in midlife?
5. What are some of the most important ways middle-aged adults in our society are expected to measure up?
6. According to historians, what were the dominant gender-role images to develop in our society? How were males and females thought to be different from each other?
7. Describe some of the limitations and problems that men and women face today in living up to gender-role ideals. What difficulties does the "complete woman" encounter?
8. What changes are occurring today in our economy that make status achievement more difficult for men and women in midlife?
9. Describe some of the ways that sexuality can be fraught with performance anxiety. How can cultural images of "sex appeal" lead to unrealistic sexual expectations between partners?

Discussion Questions

1. As a college student, how do you foresee your ability to balance future career success with marital and parenting responsibilities? Do you feel the necessity of "having it all"? If not, what will you give up?
2. Are you the offspring of a dual-career couple? If so, how do your parents juggle the responsibilities of their gender roles?
3. Do you have a parent who has lost a job? What effect did it have on his or her self-image? How did other members of the family respond?
4. Do you feel there is a greater "blurring" of the traditional gender roles now that more women are in the labor force? Why or why not?
5. What sorts of support should be available today to help working mothers balance work and family obligations? Who should be responsible for providing that support?

6. Do our institutions and other social structures make it more or less difficult today for working couples to balance work, marital, and parenting roles?
7. What are some of the ways that gender-role stereotypes have affected your own self-image? How have you handled this? Has it been a problem for you, and if so, for how long?
8. With more married women today pursuing careers outside the home, do you think we will eventually see more of their spouses opting to stay home and be "Mr. Moms"? Why or why not?

Activities

1. Examine some current issues of magazines written for working women, such as *Working Mother* and *Working Woman*. What sorts of gender-role images are extolled in these magazines? Now compare these magazines with *Cosmopolitan* and *Vogue*. How are gender images portrayed in these magazines? Are there differences in the female "ideal" between the glamour and fashion magazines and those written for working women? Discuss your findings.
2. Locate and interview a dual-career married couple who are also parents. Question them about how they cope with such a marriage. How do they balance career, marital, and parenting responsibilities? How do they decide about things like leisure activities, household chores, finances, and whose career takes precedence? Report your findings back to the class.
3. Browse through some magazines or newspapers that have a Personals section: men seeking women and women seeking men. Draw up a list of characteristics that men and women seek in each other. Are there characteristics that seem gender neutral? If so, what sorts of characteristics are they? Of what importance is age, attractiveness, and financial standing in defining an acceptable future mate/date? Report your findings back to the class.

5

Losers, Weepers:
Dilemmas of the Underclass

Probably no concept in sociology is more central to an understanding of social structure than **stratification.** We can define stratification as the ranking of persons and groups according to unequal rewards and life chances.[1] In this chapter, we examine how people and groups in our society are stratified according to income. Income is a major determinant of life chances, of one's ability to secure good health care, adequate housing, and, most important for our discussion, the educational credentials that lead in turn to well-paying jobs. A social class can be viewed as a group of people sharing similar life chances according to their positions in economic and occupational markets.

We refer to the movement of persons in and out of various class strata as **intragenerational mobility.** Social stratification is dynamic: Social and economic change can result in movement upward or downward in the class structure. Moreover, classes themselves can expand or shrink depending on how economic and social change influence the fortunes of a particular social class.

Despite the dynamics of social mobility, social classes actually try to reproduce and maintain themselves through a process known as **social reproduction.** Rituals, networks, and manipulation of political power are means by which the more privileged social classes attempt to reproduce themselves. As we shall see a bit later in the chapter, the middle class is currently not having an easy time reproducing itself.

The stratification of a complex and pluralistic society such as ours cannot be understood, however, solely in economic terms. Status groups complicate the picture and require a more sophisticated analysis. A **status**

group is made up of persons who share a common feature—such as race, gender, or ethnicity—that is ranked according to honor or social esteem. Access to economic rewards, thus to class position, is often enhanced or inhibited by membership in a status group. Persons in less-esteemed status groups, such as a minority ethnic group, can find their access to economic success either severely restricted or completely blocked. **Institutional discrimination** refers to all the structural barriers that women and racial and ethnic minorities face in establishing a desirable class position. Sexual harassment at work, hiring discrimination, and unequal public school funding are just a few examples of how status minorities are kept "in their place" and put at a disadvantage relative to elite status groups.

*   *   *

Our economic and political systems have undergone fundamental changes in recent decades. Not only have these changes altered the class structure, but they have also worsened the life chances of various status groups. Measuring up in the modern U.S. economy is increasingly difficult for those in unfavorable positions in the class and status structure.

One of the less expensive ways of identifying the values and beliefs of Americans today is to observe their automobile bumper stickers. Though many Americans appear to have difficulty articulating what they stand for or believe in, their bumper stickers allow them to display a "personal" statement about something they think they cherish. A bumper sticker that has made the rounds through various parts of the United States in recent years reads: "He Who Dies with the Most Toys Wins." It's been my experience that those bumper stickers show up most often on BMWs and Porsches.

Such stickers portray an interesting philosophy that blossomed in the 1980s and 1990s, although it had its roots much earlier in our history. For U.S. society is indeed a society of winners and losers, of haves and have-nots, of overdogs and underdogs; and though in our past it was considered unkind and in bad taste for winners to flaunt their successes, recent decades have provided unmitigated license for conspicuous consumption. In the competitive and performance struggle today, to the victors belong the toys as well as the spoils.

And how are winners and losers determined? The performance culture plays a major role in determining who gets what because in large measure winners are people who have "measured up" and succeeded: They have the best jobs, receive the best and most education, and have performed well on myriad supposedly objective tests and appraisals.

Recently, *Newsweek* magazine featured an article on the "overclass," a convenient label for a newly emerging class of the best and the brightest. They are not necessarily wealthy, but they are advantaged in ways that allow them to excel and prosper in a credential-driven, technological economy.[2]

As in most other industrial and technocratic societies, success in the United States has much to do with credentials, that is, with who can garner the most degrees and diplomas and the highest test scores and demonstrate the most "aptitude" on quantitative scales. But it would be both inaccurate and naive to maintain that the fortunes of birth have no effect on this because we know that social class, gender, and ethnicity have much to do with who gets the best start in the credentials race. Here, then, is the obvious conflict between our ideals and our practice. Though we purportedly value equality of opportunity, not everyone starts at the same place or with the same resources in the performance struggle. And though we would like to think that educational attainment, intelligence tests, scholastic aptitude tests, and other quantitative and scientific measures of ability are objective means to sort out "the best and the brightest," the evidence now points to considerable bias in favor of the Anglo male.

Americans who want to think about it are faced with an uncomfortable dilemma. On the one hand, one can argue that, at least in theory and ideal, the emphasis on quantitative, measurable, and objective performance criteria has resulted in a successful economic system that until a few decades ago was second to none. On the other hand, such an economic system, in creating a division between winners and losers, leaves many people far behind and deprived in a nation of plenty. And, ironically perhaps, even the winners cannot be all that comfortable, for as we have seen in previous chapters, the measured self is never satisfied with material gain alone, no matter how important such an achievement might be in a materialistic society. Perfection in personal appearance, parenting for success, and conformity to gender stereotypes are performance demands that make even "winners" uneasy and anxious about their lives.

However, this chapter is devoted to looking at those who are losing or have already lost in the performance struggle. We will examine the plight of those groups of Americans who, with each passing decade, find themselves farther behind in the race to measure up. For the poor, for the unemployed, for racial and ethnic minorities, and for women, the problem is not only the psychological assaults on feelings of self-worth that accompany poverty, joblessness, and homelessness. Even more important are the material deprivations suffered by the many who have no decent place to live, not enough food to eat, and no access to health care. Whether we want to admit it or not, recent years have not been good to those who lose.

Though the number of Americans living in poverty declined slightly in 1995, the fact is that about 36 million Americans live below the official poverty line.[3] Women, blacks, and Hispanics are more likely to live in poverty than are whites and males. Moreover, there is a well-documented and growing gap between the earnings of the rich and those of the poor and the middle class. For example, in 1975 the yearly earnings of a CEO at General Electric was $500,000, which equaled the income of thirty-six families earning the U.S. median income of $13,719. In 1995, a CEO at General Electric earned over $5 million, equal to the median earnings of 133 U.S. families.[4] Male workers at the low end of the labor market have seen their wages decline for more than two decades. According to Labor Secretary Robert Reich, the proportion of working families living below the poverty line increased from 7.5 percent in the late 1970s to over 11 percent in 1995.[5] And the working poor often do not qualify for safety net benefits, such as Medicaid, because their incomes, low as they are, are too high. Also, proposed budget cuts in federal spending will eliminate or reduce the few federal supports that the working poor are now receiving, such as low-income housing and job training.

Robert H. Frank and Philip J. Cook, in their recent book *The Winner-Take-All Society*, demonstrate that Americans today are competing for "fewer and bigger prizes."[6] They argue that the economy is now increasingly dominated by a winner-take-all reward structure that once applied only in sports and entertainment; that is, larger and larger rewards go to fewer and fewer people. Only the very best credentialed and able performers will be able to prosper in this kind of economy.

Some will argue that there will always be winners and losers in a highly competitive and performance-oriented economy, and there is an element of truth to such an argument. It is difficult to deny that the performance ethic has served the U.S. economy well through the years. One can say that the rigorous processes of measurement, necessary to ensure competence among a substantial number of people, have been a major reason why our society is an important creative force and is one of the most productive societies in the world.

However, two fundamental problems have emerged that threaten the future productivity and success of the economy. First, the traditional and by now well-documented problem of equal access and reward must not be ignored. In an economic system that requires more and more credentials for one to "succeed," those groups that fall short on credentials will lag farther behind in the performance struggle and are in danger of becoming a permanent underclass. Second, within the last two decades it has become increasingly obvious to many political and economic observers that the United States is in a period of economic decline. Past dreams of unlimited economic growth, prosperity, and international dominance are no longer being realized. Public attitudes reveal that many Americans are pessimistic about the future and no longer have much confidence that the economy will expand and deliver on the traditional American promises of prosperity for all who will work for it. Many are now questioning whether the American Dream is possible for them.

Indeed, both the processes and the effects of what some political economists call **deindustrialization**—a reduction in our industrial capacity and work—are well documented. The U.S. economy, which was once thought to be unequaled in its ability to generate abundant industrial jobs and to dominate international markets, now finds itself unable to generate nearly enough family-wage jobs or a competitive advantage over other industrialized nations. Moreover, **corporate downsizing**—reductions in a corporation's workforce, a phenomenon fully blossoming in the 1990s—has had adverse effects on the economic futures of thousands of persons in middle management, once the backbone of the middle class.

Deindustrialization and downsizing intertwine to produce potentially disastrous results. We must consider that there are millions of Americans who desperately need jobs that pay decent family wages and are psychologically rewarding. Yet many of these same Americans lack "performance criteria," the credentials and qualifications required for those jobs. Coupled with this is the general decline of the economy and its inability to expand and generate the sorts of work opportunities necessary to lift millions out of the underclass. As the economy continues to produce fewer high-paying jobs, the credential crunch will become all the more severe in the scramble for the lucrative jobs that remain. Whereas a few years ago a college degree was mandatory for entry into certain careers, today an MBA or better is required. And if college students are feeling pressured, what despair must be felt by the millions of Americans who have barely finished high school and have no college prospects?

The effects of deindustrialization are not encouraging. Until just very recently, the U.S. economy was experiencing a steady decline in manufacturing jobs. In their series "America: Who Stole the Dream?" journalists Donald L. Barlett and James B. Steele documented deindustrialization.[7] As imports flooded U.S. markets, the number of U.S. manufacturing jobs began a steep decline; some 2.6 million jobs have been lost since 1979. The manufacture of machine tools serves as a good example of a vanishing job market. In 1980, the U.S. was a leader in the manufacture of custom machine tools, providing some 108,000 jobs in this industry.[8] By 1995, nearly half those jobs had disappeared, leaving only 58,300 machine tool jobs available.

Corporate downsizing has had similar results for the middle class. One can hardly read a newspaper or magazine today without reading about the plans of some corporation to lop thousands of employees from its payroll. Often those being lopped are in the managerial ranks, as corporations attempt to rid themselves of excessive and redundant management. In today's economy, the "lean and mean" corporate structure is thought to be most effective in world competition.

The *New York Times* recently described the merger of Chase and Chemical banks.[9] Management predicts that in three years, 74,000 jobs will be lost as 480 bank branches are closed due to the merger. "Survivor cynicism" now describes the attitudes of those whose jobs were not lost. One executive, a business analyst with Chase for ten years, remarked: "The merger has eliminated for me a certain motivation and all risk, because this boy was a risk taker. I'm not doing that anymore."[10]

In the 1980s those losing jobs were primarily factory workers in America's heartland. In the 1990s, it is office workers on the two coasts, older and better educated workers, who are being laid off in higher numbers.

For those unemployed, underemployed, or just entering the labor market, there is now the promise of an ever expanding **service economy,** the sector of the economy that offers services rather than the production of goods. Whenever political and economic leaders boast publicly about the increase in the number of jobs, it is usually this segment of the economy they are referring to, though they rarely say so specifically. They have good reason not to. Service-sector jobs, though increasingly plentiful, are not likely to pay well or to be the prestigious jobs that adult men and women can feel they have measured up in. More often than not, service-sector jobs offer minimum wage, or barely above, and are hardly the sort of work that will enable a person to support a family, get ahead in life, or experience a sense of achievement.

Barlett and Steele, in their investigations of deindustrialization, found that many workers who lost manufacturing jobs ended up in service industries that pay barely more than minimum wage, $4.25 an hour at the time of their study.[11] Some service-sector jobs pay up to $9 per hour, but even that amounts to only $18,720 per year. Is this enough for a family to live on today?

The general decline of the industrial sector in the United States is not a by-product of the 1990s, though we hear more about it today. Basic trends toward an increase in the service sector have been noticed in the economy for some time. Between 1950 and 1976, the economy produced 1.5 times as many jobs with below-average wages as with above-average wages. And during this period, two out of every three jobs were in two basic areas: retail trade and services. These two sectors of the economy alone accounted for some 70 percent of all new jobs created from 1973 to 1980. And by the late 1970s, the increase in the number of people working in eating and drinking places was greater than the total number of workers in the steel and auto industries.[12]

Clearly, jobs and careers that are lucrative, prestigious, and satisfying will remain in short supply relative to the number of persons seeking them in today's market. Competition will be all the more fierce. In such a situation, credentials and objective qualifications will take on added significance and importance with each passing decade. Each year the "acceptable" SAT scores for entrance to the better colleges will go up, elite professional and graduate schools will seek and find students with ever higher LSAT and MCAT scores, and prospective employers will scan colleges and universities for those students with the highest GPAs and the most impressive résumés. Today, an average high school record is tantamount to failure, and a midrange SAT score is cause for suspicion about the success potential of an entering college freshman.

The issue of returns on education can be raised here. Is the learning reflected by educational credentials necessary for successful job performance, or is the requirement for credentials primarily a screen to keep certain people out of the better jobs when there is so much competition for them? The latter can be safely argued. Diplomas and credentials are handy, objective means for employers to screen people. Who can argue with a credential? Yet in recent decades the median educational level of those persons unemployed has been very close to that of those employed.[13]

There is mounting evidence that increasing educational requirements for jobs are often not linked to the performance requirements of those jobs. The cab driver with a PhD is not necessarily a fiction.

Before examining more closely the flaws and pitfalls of a credentialed society, a word about equality of opportunity is necessary. First, if qualifications and credentials are necessary for a person in our society to have any chance of career success, the question of equal access to opportunities must be raised. In the 1960s, the United States embarked on an ambitious plan to open up opportunity and mobility channels to millions of citizens who by virtue of their race, ethnicity, or penury would otherwise be left out. The general trend of social policy, at least on the national level, was to ensure that as many people as possible got a chance to measure up, to prove themselves. Reforms in access to education, aimed particularly at overcoming discrimination against blacks and members of other minorities, were instituted. Programs such as Headstart were promulgated and welcomed by reformers. In the economic and job sphere, the Office of Economic Opportunity, the Job Corps, and even the famous War on Poverty and affirmative action policies were thought to be advances in fighting unemployment and discrimination.

But such programs had only limited success. Many open-enrollment programs failed, due in part to the inability of colleges and universities to instill basic skills in those students who came to them with severely defective educational backgrounds. Affirmative action programs led to widespread hostility among those whites and males who felt they had measured up, only to find themselves shunted aside in favor of minorities with lower test scores. The effort to compensate for past injustices and unfairness to minorities was perceived by many in the majority to be unjust and unfair to them.

Supporters of the equal opportunity programs of the 1960s and 1970s now argue that disadvantaged minorities did make some notable gains and would have continued to make more in the 1970s and 1980s had not such programs been underfunded and in some cases terminated. In other words, supporters argue (and in my estimation rightly) that just as some progress in equal opportunity was being made, national policymakers shifted funding priorities to other areas (the Vietnam War and, later, huge defense outlays), and many of the social programs of the 1960s were allowed to wither away.

If by the late 1970s equality of opportunity as a national priority was a dying issue, by the 1990s it was firmly and unequivocally laid to rest as successive administrations eagerly read the last rites. Today, with the exception of some activist organizations, Americans hardly pay even lip service to the ideals of equality of opportunity, to the dream of providing greater access to minorities and the poor. In fact, we have witnessed the glorification of wealth and the virtues of private privilege. Television commercials now extol the "privileges of membership," and the unbridled consumption habits of the yuppies have been applauded and encouraged.

Since the 1970s all administrations, both Republican and Democrat, have sought to distance themselves from the "liberal" social policies of the 1960s. Instead, the War on Drugs, illegal immigration, and balancing the federal budget have become our nation's top priorities. And in a time when many families at the low end of the class structure have difficulty finding family-wage jobs, welfare reform has become a top government priority. People on welfare have become the scapegoat for failed economic policies, and the federal government seeks to restrict benefits and turn control and responsibilities over to the states.

As things stand today, a college degree—accompanied by high test scores, high GPAs, and a dynamic résumé package that no recruiter can afford to overlook—is mandatory for career success. Persons without college degrees, with the exception of those fortunate enough to find union-supported industrial jobs, are for the most part relegated to finding their economic futures in the low-paying, low-prestige, and high-turnover jobs in the service sector. The college degree has become the "union card." Without it there is little need to apply.

Yet the work that calls for a college degree does not always utilize the talents, abilities, and knowledge that the college-educated person has acquired. These are the dangers of overqualification amply documented by economic historian Harry Braverman and economist Ivar Berg, among others. Braverman, for example, has demonstrated that many highly educated people cannot find jobs that require the level of education they have achieved.[14] Though they have measured up educationally, such persons find themselves in jobs that are not commensurate with their knowledge and skills. And Ivar Berg pointed out some time ago the tenuous connection between education and jobs in U.S. society.[15] In a detailed study of job training, Berg found that over time the tendency is for substantial numbers of people to end up in jobs that utilize less education than they have obtained. And in certain fields, such as insurance sales, persons with less education actually performed better at their work and earned more money. Berg also discovered that organizations and companies often hire people with high degrees of education but fail to promote them to the level where their education is needed. Such persons often quit because they realize that their superior education is not being fully utilized.

Nevertheless, in a society where credentials count for so much in being hired in the first place, one is not well-advised to act on the basis of the research of people like Ivar Berg. Instead, one ought to get a degree and make the best of it because a college degree remains the "measuring rod" of career potential in much of today's labor market. We have seen the power of credentials and measurable qualifications; we must now look at the plight of the uncredentialed and those who occupy the most disadvantaged positions in the performance struggle.

Women

The feminist movement has done much to raise awareness of the special plight of women in the United States today. We have especially been made to recognize the economic hardships suffered not only by single women but also by women who through divorce or separation now must raise families on their own.

The women we might refer to as "traditional" are an interesting and often tragic case in point. Millions of women have been and continue to be socialized to define their femininity within the confines of marriage and family, urged to find their identity and fulfillment as good mothers and wives. These women lived by a traditional and historic but now largely defunct social compact that provided that their husbands would bring home a family wage. Being supported, these women would keep the home and be the primary nurturer of children. Such women sought, and many continue to seek, to measure up as good wives and mothers, gauging both their ability and their success within their role by the happiness and contentment of their husbands and children. More often than not, traditional women postponed their education beyond the high school minimum, as well as work outside the home, until later years, after the children had grown. Basking in their husband's educational and career attainments, traditional women traded their own attainments for the security of a lifelong commitment to a spouse who would always provide. After all, it was her performance as wife and mother that counted most, and many women never dreamed that the bubble could burst.

As Barbara Ehrenreich has pointed out, these women never anticipated the rapid erosion of the traditional social compact that followed the decrease in the family-wage system.[16] Equally important, movements such as modern growth psychology would tell men that what counted most in life was neither loyalty nor commitment but how they felt and how they were growing as persons. More to the point, modern psychology was, in effect, telling men that if they were in a marriage that did not give them the freedom and space to grow and develop their fullest emotional and psychological potential, then it was time to change, to find a new partner in a more dynamic and challenging relationship. The male in midlife crisis was portrayed in both academic and popular imagery as the victim of a stifling and stultifying marriage and home life. One of the cures was to leave.

This is an all-too-familiar scenario to traditional women, thousands of whom found themselves separated and divorced after years of marriage. Left alone to fend for themselves and their children, these women soon discovered that their postponed educations and work careers were their chief liability. What was once a loving sacrifice to a husband's ambition now hung heavily as they realized just how difficult it is to pursue an education in midlife or to secure a high-paying job without impeccable credentials. Very often it is these women who experience downward mobility; some of them will join the ranks of the new poor.

Ruth Sidel's *Women and Children Last*[17] and Katherine S. Newman's *Falling from Grace*[18] have portrayed effectively how women's economic fortunes decline with divorce. Ruth Sidel has written one of the best books on women and poverty, and I will not attempt to duplicate her efforts here. But I would like to rely on some of her research to bring home certain points. Sidel describes the "new poor" as those women who sink into poverty as they assume the status of single parent. Both factors—singleness and parenthood—are involved, and it makes little difference which comes first.

Often the decline into poverty is dramatic and traumatic, especially for middle-class women who have enjoyed a secure existence for many years. Sidel relates the experiences of a woman in her survey who, after twenty-three years of marriage, thirteen pregnancies, and eight children, was informed by her husband that he "wanted out" in order to pursue his love for another woman.[19] She descended from a family income of $70,000 per year to $7,000. She faced the reality of living on occasional court-mandated child support payments (her husband left his job as well). As this source of income quickly dried up, she was forced to sell her household appliances to live, and shortly after lost her home to a bank foreclosure. Within a year and a half of her divorce, this mother of eight children was poor.

While not all divorced, middle-class women will succumb to poverty as rapidly and dramatically as this woman did, the fact remains that hers is not an isolated case. Indeed, thousands of women can identify with her plight. Families headed by a single mother had a poverty rate of 34.9 percent in 1992,[20] and families headed by women constituted some 53 percent of all poor families.

What about those women who pursue an education as an avenue to upward career mobility or as a hedge against divorce and the peril of single parenting? Here we find an interesting dilemma for women, one that calls into question the ideals surrounding credentials. In general, women do not enjoy the same returns on their education as men. At any level of educational attainment, women earn roughly 60 percent to 70 percent of what men do.[21] In fact, many educated women have lower incomes than do men with less education. For example, according to 1992 U.S. Census data, college-educated women can expect to earn only slightly more than a high school–educated man ($26,241 compared to $24,148 per year),[22] which does not say much for encouraging women to measure up in the college classroom as a means of getting ahead. While these women will earn more than women with less education, the income gap between their incomes and men's will only narrow as discrimination practices are discontinued.

This is not to say that women shouldn't acquire all the education they possibly can, because for the divorced woman with children the chances of avoiding sustained poverty or near-poverty will be greater if she has a college degree and career experience. But even educated women will be less well off than men and thus less able to provide for the children than men, given the present structure of sex discrimination in earnings. Women with few educational credentials are much more likely to be pushed into the service sector of the economy, which, as already noted, pays less and offers few opportunities for upward career mobility.

A paradox for women today is that while more women are entering the workforce high-paying jobs are growing scarce. Barlett and Steele discovered that, except for well-educated women in the professional or middle class, most women pursue jobs in the service sector: in retail sales, as clerks, as nurse's aides, and so on.[23] In 1995, there were over 6 million adults earning between $4.25 and $5.99 per hour. Some 67 percent of these adults were women.[24] And what about the future? As more women enter the labor force, what kinds of jobs will be in demand in the decades ahead? According to the Department of Labor, these are the top five jobs in growth potential: cashiers, janitors/cleaners, retail sales clerks, waiters/ waitresses, and registered nurses. In four of these five job categories, men earn more than women, but even more important, the median earnings in these occupations for women would qualify a family of four for the earned-income tax credit.[25] In other words, they would be among the working poor.

Black Americans

Black Americans make up 12 percent of the U.S. population, thus making this group our country's largest minority group. They have also found themselves at a distinct disadvantage in competing in today's economy, though their position in society has gotten both better and worse.

With respect to educational attainment, black Americans have made impressive gains and have narrowed the gap with white Americans considerably. For instance, by 1991 the median years of schooling for both blacks and whites were nearly equal: roughly twelve years for each group.[26] While only 20 percent of blacks completed high school in 1960, today nearly 87 percent graduate from high school.

However, a significant gap remains when it comes to completing college. In fact, since 1970, the percent of black students enrolled in four-year colleges has declined. Whites are twice as likely to finish college than are blacks or Hispanics. The focus of federal aid to college students has changed to favor middle-class white students.

A decade ago, educator Stan Warren spoke of a "lost generation" of black college students, citing statistics that show that the number of black students attending college may have declined by 20 percent during the 1980s.[27] And this was at a time when more blacks were completing high school and were posting steady increases in ACT and SAT scores.

Despite gains among black Americans in median levels of education, they are not close to attaining economic equality. Race is still an important factor dampening wage levels.[28] Black families have always earned less income on the average than white families, and continue to do so despite gains in black educational attainment. For example, in 1960 black family income was 55 percent of white family income. In 1991, when median years of schooling for whites and blacks were nearly equal, black family income was still only 55 percent of white family income. Blacks are three times as likely to be poor as whites.

Though the picture of the black middle-class is less bleak, in that the percentage of black middle-class families has doubled in recent years, the fact remains that 26 percent of all black families have an income of less than $10,000 per year. This fact points to the growing underclass to be found in U.S. urban "hyperghettos" where hopelessness and crime often abound. However, rural blacks, especially black females, are among the poorest groups to be found in our society.

Hispanics

Hispanic American is a broad category whose subgroups include Mexican Americans, Puerto Ricans, Cubans, and others with origins in Central and Latin America.[29] Hispanics make up nearly 10 percent of the current population of the United States, and predictions are that they will be the largest U.S. minority group by the year 2020.

Many Hispanic Americans live near or below the poverty line. Their education and job skills put them at a severe disadvantage. In 1991, median family income for Hispanics was $23,895, or 63 percent of median white family income,[30] and 26 percent of all Hispanic families lived in poverty, more than three times the rate of white families. Actually, a higher percentage of Hispanic families lived in poverty in 1991 than in 1980: 26.5 percent compared to 23.2 percent. In late 1996, the *New York Times* reported that, for the first time, a higher proportion of Hispanics than of blacks were officially defined as poor.[31] And though median family income for both whites and blacks rose in 1995, median family income declined by 5 percent for Hispanics.

Educationally, Hispanics are not faring well either. For example, only 53 percent of Hispanics completed high school in 1992.[32] Their high school drop-out rate is twice as high as that of blacks and three times that of whites. Within the Hispanic groups, Mexican Americans, who make up 60 percent of all Hispanics in the United States, have struggled even more educationally. In 1992, only 45.2 percent of Mexican Americans over the age of twenty-five had completed high school, and only 6 percent had had four years or more of college. Economically, more than 27 percent of Mexican American families lived in poverty. Many Mexican Americans work in low-paying jobs such as migrant farm labor, or in urban sweatshops.[33]

We can see here the distinct possibility of an emerging and relatively permanent **underclass**—a class of people who acquire less education and whose employment opportunities are restricted—in the United States as two processes appear to have been set in motion. In general, returns on education are greater for whites (especially males) than for blacks and

probably for other minorities. And since the educational level of the unemployed is not significantly lower than that of the employed, it is un-
likely that substantial increases in education will have a profound effect on
reducing black unemployment. What is likely to happen is that ghetto
schools will continue to have high drop-out rates, though the overall rate
of high school graduation among blacks is improving. And as Warren and
others have indicated, minority enrollment is decreasing on college campuses, giving white students all the greater competitive advantage for
those high-paying, prestigious jobs that require a college degree.

The traditional avenues to upward mobility in U.S. society, education
and an expanding industrial economy, are clearly not as accessible as they
have been in the past. We are witnessing a gradual polarization between a
privileged class composed mainly of middle- and upper-class whites who
are well educated and highly credentialed, and an underclass composed
mainly of blacks and other minorities who are less educated and whose
educations are worth less relative to whites. The privileged white group
will be able to feel they have measured up as they use their college credentials to pursue high-paying and prestigious careers. The minority underclass will continue to occupy the lowest rungs of the occupational ladder, working at jobs that will rarely lift them out of inner-city housing
projects.

The Credential Spiral

It is evident that **credential inflation** has replaced economic inflation as
one of our most pressing problems. As sociologist Randall Collins
pointed out in his study of education and stratification, education was the
"weapon" traditionally used to obtain privilege in U.S. society.[34] Credentials (degrees, diplomas, and so on) were a means of gaining access to desired goods. Today, however, the performance ethic in education has produced a high level of credential inflation, so that one's education is not
worth as much as it once was. So many people are now educated at high
levels, due to the massive expansion of the educational system, that the
impact of education on inequality is becoming negligible.

Blacks and members of other ethnic minorities are becoming victims of
a cruel hoax. For just as they increased their high school graduation rates
to within striking distance of whites, high school diplomas no longer
counted as a passport to high-paying jobs and honorable careers.

Today, a career (outside the unionized, industrial sector, which is not expanding rapidly enough to absorb large numbers of minorities) that a person can feel good about requires at least one college degree. As noted earlier, for various reasons (not all of them clear), blacks are less likely to pursue a college degree and graduate, yet such a credential is nearly mandatory. And the whites who increasingly populate the college campus, in an atmosphere where credential mania proliferates and intensifies, gain most of the advantages in competing for lucrative careers. If the credential spiral continues, the prospects do not look good for minorities in the decades ahead unless there is a major overhaul in funding for education (especially for higher education) or a reevaluation of how we look at qualifications for jobs and careers. Perhaps only the latter can assure greater equality and lead to a more humane way of allocating work in our society.

Credentialing in the United States is reaching the point where completing an education no longer assures success. Some think that private, elite schools offer the best educational advantages for those who really desire to compete successfully for our society's most rewarding careers. And admission to the elite private colleges is often a matter of having proved oneself at private high school and elementary schools. If this isn't enough, for parents concerned that their children have a leg up on other children there are now elite, private preschools that offer the very best in reading instruction, media centers, and computer facilities.

But if an elite private education is required for success, even middle-class and relatively affluent families cannot be all that certain that their children can compete successfully for the best educational credentials that communities have to offer. Whether they are correct or not, some middle-class parents feel that their children's journey to Yale or Princeton must begin in the best private schools, even in elite and private preschools. "Preschool panic" describes the feeling of mothers in an affluent section of Atlanta, Georgia, who were anxious about whether one of the handful of elite private preschools would admit their two-year-olds.[35] Trying to give their toddlers every advantage in a highly selective admissions process, some mothers offered to change religion if it meant getting their child admitted to a particular private school. Moreover, parents willingly subjected their two- and three-year-olds to psychological and intelligence tests as well as intensive interviews with admissions officials to winnow out the brightest and most talented youngsters from the merely intelligent and average. Likewise, parents considered yearly tuition charges of up to $4,656 a worthwhile investment in their preschooler's educational future.

Obviously, even some affluent families do not feel secure in their ability to provide their children all the advantages. If affluent parents are worrying about whether their child has what it takes for a private, elite preschool, how can those children born into poverty or into the lower class hope to succeed when private and elite educations are beyond them financially and otherwise? At the college level, even public education costs are increasing at a rate higher than the annual rate of inflation. And at the secondary and primary level, how can public school systems, often overcrowded, understaffed, and inadequately funded, offer the kind of experiences that private schools do?

Middle-class parents educating their children in public schools recognize the dilemma. In 1995 *Time* magazine featured the school district of Brookline, Massachusetts. For many years, Brookline cherished the principle of school equity, which held that all the public schools should be funded and equipped at comparable levels. Today, however, parents at some schools fear their children will not be able to learn on the most sophisticated computer equipment, thus putting them at a competitive disadvantage. One school initiated its own fund drive and raised over $30,000 to purchase twenty-six Apple computers.[36] While the school budgets in many public school districts are shrinking due to tax cuts, affluent parents stand ready to help their own children's public school through private fund drives. And why wouldn't they?

It is not my intention to oversimplify or overgeneralize here, as we know that many students from the public school system "succeed" and that some students from elite schools don't. And maybe that is the larger point. There is nothing inherent in this spiraling credential race that assures that the most able or the most hardworking or dedicated of our young people are going to succeed and achieve. Nor is there much in educational credentials themselves that guarantees that what has been taught or learned is valuable in helping us deal with the critical issues of our time. There is precious little proof that these credentials really mean anything with respect to eventual success, ability, or productivity. Though in general children from affluent families appear to have advantages in attending private schools, their advantage is limited primarily to duplicating their parents' level of achievement, not necessarily surpassing it. And such children, despite their relative affluence, might not receive an education that permits them a higher level of self-knowledge, worldly insight, or productivity. By allowing a credentialing system to replicate the class structure, we are not using our vast educational system to accomplish its more important function of enabling all young people to achieve greater productivity, self-mastery, and sensitivity to issues of human equality and cooperation. In short, education today has to be defined more broadly than as a way to gain academic credentials necessary for careers.

There is some evidence that a century or more ago, our democratic ethos and less-complex economy combined to create a work environment such that minimum credentials in most fields were sufficient for a start in life. Success, productivity, reliability, resourcefulness, and other work traits were tested on the job. After all, the so-called self-made men and women were often cultural heroes in America, those held up as role models for a younger generation. There was rampant race, gender, and ethnic discrimination, but education in its present form has failed to eliminate such discrimination and has added the more subtle discrimination of credentials. At least in ideology, and to some degree in practice, in past generations people were able to rise and fall on their own abilities, aside from any educational attainments they might have acquired.

Our obsession with academic credentials, test scores, grades, and so on assures us of little beyond the replication of the class structure. Such criteria may give corporate recruiters and graduate schools a sense that they are selecting the best people, but actually there is little way of knowing whether they are or not.

I'm reminded of a television commercial of several years ago that portrayed a young Abraham Lincoln in a modern employment office seeking a job. The employment official began to question Lincoln about his educational background. Lincoln soon found himself hard-pressed to present any qualifications for a job the agency might offer. Shaking his head sadly, the employment officer lamented that while he would like to help him, there was little that Lincoln qualified for. His résumé was so incomplete. The commercial message was on behalf of a metropolitan area school that offered the right kind of degrees and educational preparation for career success in today's world.

Whether or not Lincoln would be a success in modern culture is beside the point. Fortunately, he lived in an era where ability, productivity, and competence were not so neatly packaged. Lincoln could prove himself as a leader without the aid of intelligence tests, curriculum specialists, and educational bureaucrats. Lincoln's superior abilities and talents were allowed to evolve and flourish in the practical routines of everyday life. Lincoln and others of his age were permitted the luxury that too few people experience today (especially young people): to search for and discover their abilities in meeting the demand of the day, not in measuring up in quantified ways to educational standards and programs often remote from practical and worldly concerns.

If educational credentials are truly an adequate means of preparing people to be resourceful, creative, and productive in the world, and not mostly a mechanism for allocating privilege, why does there appear to be such a crisis in leadership and productivity in our society? If the best and most able are supposed to reach the top in this kind of system, why don't they? Witness in recent years the public dismay with leadership in government, economy, and even religion. What is the record in the United States? It is one of gradual decline in economic productivity and quality of work while industrial leaders pursue short-term maximization of profits. Few economic leaders appear to have workable, humane, and efficient solutions to the problem of reindustrializing our society, and many financial leaders on Wall Street seem to be committed to the most short-sighted greed and even dishonest trading and secrecy. Our political leaders lack the courage to be more concerned with substance than image. Most of them are led in whatever direction public opinion polls point. Moreover, recent decades have brought us nearly unprecedented levels of political chicanery, fraud, and corruption. Watergate apparently was only the beginning, not the culmination, of modern high-level government corruption. And we have found little to give us confidence in certain religious leaders, who themselves have engaged in the most blatant immorality and deceit. This is all part of the record of top leadership in the United States, though there are numerous exceptions and there are many able, talented, and productive people in government service, industry, and religious organizations. But surely we can do better in providing opportunities for more people to utilize their productive capacity, creativity, and resourcefulness. Presently we permit credentials and "measured" educational achievements to substitute for more effective and fair means to ensure that the most capable people have a chance to become leaders and to serve.

Are we not consigning a significant and growing portion of our population to poverty and neglect without even furnishing them real opportunities to develop their talents? Is it not self-destructive to continue to use supposedly objective and predictive educational tests and measures to screen out people whose abilities and potentials do not test well or who are not "early advantaged?" One wonders how much needed talent, integrity, and resourcefulness slips through the cracks of an educational system devoted to testing, curriculum paths, degree programs, and measurable results. How much talent among the poor, among minorities, who do not always test well, are we losing and neglecting at a time when the complexity of national and world issues requires the very best efforts of everyone?

Empathy Failure

Several years ago, psychologist William Ryan argued that Americans are often given to **blaming the victim** of social problems for his or her troubles.[37] That is, rather than searching for fundamental causes of social problems, we give the responsibility to the victim for his or her personal, psychological, and subcultural inadequacies.

We see examples of victim blaming most readily in attitudes toward the poor and minorities: "Why are they poor, and why do they suffer? Because," we answer "they don't work hard enough; they drop out of school; they lack the psychological need to achieve." The list of personal inadequacies cited goes on. And once we have blamed the victim, we aren't required to look any deeper into our cultural values, social structures, or institutional arrangements as sources of poverty and human neglect. Having placed the blame, problems of class inequality need no longer concern us.

No one has illustrated this phenomenon much better than Lillian B. Rubin in her book *Families on the Fault Line*.[38] In a provocative chapter entitled "Is This a White Country or What?" Rubin's interviews with white working-class families reveal deep resentment toward people of color in our society. The working class is vulnerable; they have suffered significantly during the nation's deindustrialization. In their pain, however, they tend to blame minorities of color for their own job losses and economic insecurities. Rather than seeing their economic dilemmas as a result of the structural contradictions of late capitalism, they see their real enemies as the "immigrants" who are taking their jobs and getting preferential treatment in U.S. institutions. And this is also the view expressed by our country's leading political figures, who warn us daily of the dangers of the "illegal immigrant."

I would like to place victim blaming in the larger context of **empathy failure,** which is our learned inability to empathize with the victims of social injustice and inequality. And I use the term "learned" because there are so few social supports or opportunities for people to develop empathetic consciousness. If our more natural response is to empathize with the plight of fellow human beings, in our culture we must *learn* not to. In a society of winners and losers, we are taught to emulate the winners and avoid the losers. Whatever charitable impulses we might have toward losers is channeled into support for organizations such as United Way or even into government welfare programs—as long as they don't cost too much. In effect, "charitable work" is meant to take care of the losers and mitigate against the worst excesses of a highly competitive system.

This sort of attitude, as pervasive as it is today, is not conducive to a productive society, and it is probably inimical to some of our traditions of democratic opportunity. The performance ethic in the economy and in education, and its attendant emphasis on supposedly objective screening of who gets ahead, has resulted in an unnecessary and unproductive structure of winners and losers. Unlike in the past, however, the losers are dangerously close to becoming a permanent class, defying the dream that losers can eventually catch up and become winners. When degrees, diplomas, and test scores become the criteria for allocating privilege, credential inflation threatens the morality of our system.

If we are to live up to democratic ideals and meet the practical realities of the world we live in, we must reward and encourage real productivity and resourcefulness. We cannot permit the credential spiral to continue unabated. A compassionate response to the losers requires us to reexamine our economic and educational institutions and how we allocate careers and positions of leadership. A system of winners and losers can no longer guarantee the economic and political future of our society.

Key Terms

1. Stratification
2. Intragenerational Mobility
3. Social Reproduction
4. Status Groups
5. Institutional Discrimination
6. Deindustrialization
7. Corporate Downsizing
8. Service Economy
9. Underclass
10. Credential Inflation
11. Blaming the Victim
12. Empathy Failure

Review Questions

1. What is deindustrialization? What has been the impact of deindustrialization on American class mobility?
2. What is corporate downsizing? How has corporate downsizing affected the life chances of America's middle class?
3. What is meant by the service economy? What has been the impact of the growing service economy on the American class structure?
4. What problems do working women face in today's economy? Which women are most vulnerable to downward mobility? Why?
5. What are the gains and losses made by America's black families today? What role does education play in the social mobility of blacks?
6. How have Hispanics fared in the contemporary American economy? What has been the impact of educational attainment on Hispanic economic success?
7. Why do many Americans blame the victims of economic injustice rather than economic policies and institutions?

Discussion Questions

1. What role should federal policy play in reducing economic injustice in the United States?
2. How can educational opportunities be expanded for members of racial and ethnic minorities?
3. Do you feel that members of your generation will match or surpass the class standing of your parents' generation? Why or why not?
4. What public and economic policies should be devised to reduce corporate downsizing and deindustrialization? Who should take more responsibility for these policies, government or private economic organizations?
5. Are educational institutions today adequately preparing students to succeed in the future economy? Why or why not?
6. What can U.S. cities do today to address the educational and economic needs of their ghetto underclass? Is this an urban problem or a national problem?
7. What are you doing personally to improve your chances for economic success? How important is economic success to you?

Activities

1. Interview a small sample of faculty, students, and staff at your college or university. Inquire about their views concerning affirmative action. Do they feel

affirmative action is just or effective? Which persons in your sample were most likely and which were least likely to support affirmative action policies? How do you account for this? Report your findings back to the class.

2. Interview some of the admissions staff at your college or university. Ask them what they are doing to recruit racial and ethnic minority students. Have they been successful? What problems do they face? Report your findings back to the class.

3. Locate a magazine or newspaper article that deals with either corporate downsizing, deindustrialization, or the expanding service industry. Does the article pose any problems associated with this economic trend? If so, what problems are addressed? Does the article pose any solutions? Is the tone of the article pessimistic, optimistic, or neutral? Does it imply anything for the future of the nation's economy or for its class/status structure? Summarize your article and report on it to the class.

Constructing a New Vision: The Emergence of the Productive Self

A central tenet of sociology is that social and cultural change are not only possible but probable. And where needed changes seem to be occurring too slowly, we have the capability to speed up the process. I would like to introduce this final chapter by looking at two ways we can bring about social and cultural change.

C. Wright Mills argued that the promise of sociology is that through the sociological imagination individuals can effect social change. When people can connect their individual biographies with historical moments, then change is possible.[1] As Mills put it, the fact that we live means that we contribute, whether greatly or minutely, to the shaping of our society and its history.[2] When we can see the intersection of our lives with the larger social institutions and their transformations, we develop a self-consciousness. We can view ourselves as outsiders and see our world more objectively. The self and the social world can become objects, not only to be seen and known but to be imagined in new ways, as things that can be acted upon and changed. The sociological imagination allows its possessor to take charge of the self and history, to become an agent of social change.

The second aspect of human agency is that individuals do act on society as forces in their own right; society is not something that exists only as an external force. Granted, few of us will be the "movers and shakers" of great cultural change. But in our daily interactions with others, in what we do and in how we think and feel, we give shape and substance to society. As sociologist David Newman put it: "Communication is what holds society together."[3] It is through daily communication among people that society is affirmed, made real, and altered. As social communicators, we give shape and meaning to the social order. Thus, change is always possible in our patterns of communication and interaction. When we act, think, and talk differently, society is forever altered.

In this last chapter of *Measuring Up*, we will see how a change in self-hood and cultural orientation is possible if we think, act, and speak about things in new terms.

*   *   *

As U.S. society faces the new century, certain choices about our future are possible. We can continue to be shaped by the performance ethic, living a half-life of measured conformity. Or we can begin to press for fundamental changes in cultural orientation and value in the hope of arriving at a new kind of selfhood, one that is less conformist and measured, a self that is more authentic and genuinely free.

I would like to offer two visions of self- and cultural orientation, presented as two options for the future of life in the United States. The vision in force today encourages a selfhood I've been calling the measured self, formed as a response to the demands of the performance ethic. The new vision promotes the productive self, to be shaped by an emerging cultural orientation that we can call the productive ethic, an idea similar to the productive orientation suggested by Erich Fromm in the 1950s.[4]

The Present Vision

Americans' characters and personalities are influenced heavily by a cultural performance ethic that produces all sorts of standards for human assessment and measurement, and the measured self is a direct outgrowth of the performance culture. It is an identity and sense of self expressed in performance terms: how well one is doing on a host of measured competences, statuses, and traits.

Looking at the effects of the performance ethic through the life course, we first saw the workings of the performance ethic in the lives of toddlers and their parents. We examined the pressure on young children to perform well at early ages on developmental tasks, growth activities, standardized tests, grades, and aptitude assessments. Parents of young children were portrayed as willing victims of the performance culture as their anxiety increased about their parenting skills. In seeing to it that their children measure up to myriad psychological, educational, and developmental norms, parents push and prod their offspring to show signs of future success and potential.

We saw next that young people and adolescents growing up in a culture dominated by the performance ethic are virtually robbed of their youth and innocence as the pressures to conform to quantitative standards increase with each passing year. Since school life shapes so much of the identity of youth in our culture, measures of educational success, aptitude, and achievement set the standards of normalcy and adjustment among the young. Adolescents are thus less free to set their own life agendas, to explore their own interests and values, and to define their own purposes. Navigating in a performance culture that permits little latitude for error or failure, young people must meet the externally imposed standards of a vastly extended school system (in the form of grades, test scores, and so on) if they hope to succeed in the work settings they will face as adults.

Moreover, young people find little respite from their overly structured, school-saturated lives in the hedonistic peer group activities toward which they inevitably gravitate. For the peer group itself is heavily inundated with mass culture and consumerism and fails to provide a haven for young people from the performance pressures of school. Instead, peer group life centers around another highly competitive arena, that of fashion, looks, coolness, and popularity. Caught between the paralyzing effects of the peer subculture and the performance pressure generated by the school system, many young people face the uncomfortable reality of not measuring up in either.

Adults in their middle years face the most severe performance pressures, pressures that produce the most desperate expression of the measured self. It is in midlife that adults are expected to prove they have what it takes to measure up as men and women, spouses and parents, and career-oriented people. Having neither their future before them, as they did in their youth, nor their past accomplishments to boast about, as they might when older, they realize that only a few short years are theirs in which to accomplish all that the performance culture requires of them. The adult years, especially for those in the middle and professional classes, are fraught with the anxieties attendant on achieving success in several areas of life.

Witness the dilemma of the contemporary middle-class "complete woman," who is trying to live up to the demands of her gender to be a sexy, slim, attractive wife and an involved, caring parent, all the while meeting the performance demands of the career she has chosen. Being a sexy, slim wife might mean devoting more time to the exercise spa than to PTA meetings, to say nothing of whether she would forgo the longer hours at the office necessary if she is to be considered for her next promotion.

Middle-class men, as well, experience the contradictory pressures of being aggressive, competitive males in the economic arena, striving for upward career mobility and financial success, yet somehow living up to new standards of parenthood as they attempt to give "quality time" to their children. In their desperate quest to "have it all," middle-class men often face the reality that, as males, economic success is the only true measure of their self-worth.

And finally, we have seen how the performance ethic in education and the workplace has resulted in an overcredentialed society in which diplomas and degrees and test scores become the major screening devices for allocating economic and educational privilege. Performance on ostensibly neutral and objective criteria becomes a major determinant of who gets what. This supposedly meritocratic system masks the underlying class, ethnic, and race inequalities that continue to exist in our society. The result is that Americans soon learn to blame the losers in the performance struggle, feeling that, after all, the poor and the uneducated are at fault for failing to measure up to performance norms. The performance culture allows winners to take pride in being the authors of their own successes, attributing them to their own educational merits and objective abilities, while censuring the losers for their lack of ability.

Moreover, the spiral of credentials means that increasing emphasis will be placed on credentials that are ever more difficult to obtain for economic success. As whites and males of the middle and professional classes continue to enjoy the benefits of educational privilege (college and professional school), they will secure for themselves the greatest economic privilege. We have witnessed in the 1990s the emergence of an underclass, in danger of being permanently mired in an educational system that discriminates against them on test scores and grades, and an economic system that shuts them out from the more favored positions on the basis of credentials. The underclass is caught in a vicious performance struggle in which their failure to measure up educationally seals their economic fate.

The present vision is characterized by a measured self that results from a cultural orientation emphasizing measured performance. The measured self is dependent on the judgment of others (such as peer groups, teachers, parents, bosses); it is a selfhood that occasionally becomes nearly comfortable. For it is interesting to note that beauty pageants never lack for entrants; organizational leaders willingly submit to all sorts of assessments and evaluations; diet, fitness, and beauty magazines sell by the millions; and the ETS at Princeton continues to thrive and prosper.

In a selfhood that is dependent on the judgment of others, a personality type emerges that is passive, conformist, and anxious for approval. People are less likely to trust their own experiences and judgments; somehow their personal and unique habits, traditions, and experiences are suspect and not highly valued. There results an exaltation of the external in which gender stereotypes are accepted as meaningful and real; grades and test scores become equated with education; and expert advice in the fields of psychology, medicine, and even astrology are regarded as synonymous with sound personal judgment.

Rooted in such twentieth-century phenomena as consumerism, bureaucratic rationality, scientism, and professionalism, the performance ethic took shape as a major cultural orientation of our time. The measured self became a model character of the present, reaching its culmination in the 1990s, a decade characterized by mass consumerism, credentialism, and professionalism. Many persons might be comfortable with their measured selves, which presents the haunting prospect that people can be secure in their unfreedom. Such was the vision so aptly described by Erich Fromm in his work on alienation and freedom.[5]

Despite the possibility that many people learn to find some sense of comfort and security in the measured self, I think it is worthwhile to explore a new vision of personality and cultural orientation in the decades to come. It is worth considering, also, how changes in our social structure, in how we accomplish things, can lead to new possibilities of selfhood.

A New Vision

The present is ripe with the possibility of imagining new ways of being, thinking, and acting. What these new alternatives might be is open to speculation, but it is fitting that I close this book by offering my insights into the direction that some of these changes might take, that is, by exercising my sociological imagination.

Changes in cultural orientations and character come very slowly and haltingly, but it is timely to envision new forms of selfhood if Americans are going to be more genuinely free to live the kinds of lives that make them more fully human. An agenda for the late 1990s and beyond must include new ways of looking at ourselves as parents, teachers, workers, and, even more broadly, as men and women.

I would like to set up the possibilities and potentials of a new sense of selfhood that I will call the "productive self." The identification here is built upon and extends the idea of the "productive orientation" developed by Erich Fromm in his book *The Sane Society*. But I'm not speaking here as much about a cultural orientation as about a kind of selfhood, about a way of reorienting how we see ourselves, and about the kind of persons we could become. Cultural orientation is included, to be sure, for much of selfhood is derived from culture. I'm describing the productive self not only as the result of a different orientation but also as a new possibility for people to be more fully human and less alienated. The **productive self** will refer to a self whose life is defined by a person's ability to release the creative, productive resources that lie within them. The productive self will draw on inner sources of direction, action, and creativity that can unleash a greater sense of human freedom and liberation.

The Productive Self

In developing the idea of the productive self, I have benefited greatly from the early work of Erich Fromm, who argued that the solution to the problems of the human condition is productive activity.[6] I consider Fromm's theory to be as valid and fresh today as it was in the 1950s, and I suggest that modern social critics and planners would do well to read carefully Fromm's criteria for a sane society.

People have a deep-seated need to engage in their world productively and actively. Humans are creative and need to express that creativity in much, perhaps all, that they do. The productive self wants to shape and build and at the same time to see something of the self in the world that is being formed. The productive self desires a more direct and tangible connection between effort and value; actions are taken because they are possible and worthwhile and in touch with human wants and needs. At whatever age in life, regardless of gender, race, or class, people fundamentally desire to live and work productively in freedom. The productive self is actualized in building and creating the world rather than in merely reacting to external demands and pressures to conform or in seeking approval. Whereas the measured self is passive, reactive, approval-oriented, and mistrustful of its own judgments and experiences, the productive self is active, inner-directed, self-reliant, and constructive.

How can we give shape and substance to this productive self? Where are changes in American culture most necessary to allow the productive self to take root and flourish? We will examine three institutions: family, education, and economy/work.

Family

There is a certain danger in generalizing about family life and in thinking that only one type of family exists, for there is no single type of American family; thus, admonitions about the future of "the family" are both suspect and inaccurate. Recognizing this and limiting my remarks essentially to the middle and professional classes, I would like to probe into new directions and emphases for family life.

Christopher Lasch, in his description of family life in Western society, provides a cogent analysis of the demise of parenting in the modern world.[7] Lasch argues that just as the Industrial Revolution and new theories of scientific management devalued the knowledge and skills of workers, so too did industrialism extend control over people's private lives as medical, psychological, and educational experts began to devalue the knowledge and skills of parents. "The proliferation of medical and psychiatric advice undermines parental confidence at the same time that it encourages a vastly inflated idea of the importance of child-rearing techniques and the responsibility of their failure."[8] Nowhere is this more in evidence today in than in the middle class.

Trusting neither in their own intuitions nor in their own experiences, middle-class parents become almost completely other directed, approval oriented, dependent, and anxious. Fearing they will fail themselves as they fail their children, they anxiously await the latest pronouncements of pediatricians, psychiatrists, and child-guidance experts. Is it any wonder that their children become in turn approval oriented, conformist, and anxious about their own abilities? How can children become productive and resourceful and confident in their own creative capabilities when their parents have so little confidence in their own?

In reading through a variety of books giving advice on child-rearing, I had two reactions: First, there is an overabundance of information about techniques, skills, and approaches in raising children, enough to confuse rather than enlighten. But, second, I also found that much of the expert, detailed advice could be distilled into a few basic ideas. Most advice givers encourage parents to treat their children with respect, to encourage open communication, to employ firm discipline, and to give lots of encouragement. These suggestions hardly appear to be so esoteric, scientific, or complex that the average parent couldn't grasp them.

In fact, these basic components of parenting are consistent with a more productive orientation toward parenting itself. What is implied here is that in establishing a sense of mutual respect, parents are in effect allowing children to engage in their own maturing, permitting them to grow, create something of themselves and for themselves in a world where they feel secure, cared for, important, and respected. Such an environment is not that difficult to establish and is within the competences of most mature adults.

Despite the information in countless magazines, advice columns, and books, parents do not have to be all things to their children; there is no one "correct" method of raising children, and parents cannot be held solely responsible for their children's outcomes. Moreover, there is nothing healthy or constructive in any formula that guarantees success in raising children to achieve.

The trap is that in the present vision, dominated as it is by the performance ethic, successful parenting is synonymous with raising children to be achievement oriented. Parents are admonished to nurture their children to make good, especially in ways that can be objectively measured and compared, such as grades, test scores, and batting averages.

In the new vision, in which the productive ethic is encouraged and the productive self is allowed to flourish, parenting-for-success isn't the ultimate goal of parenting, nor is it important that parents learn the scientific techniques for motivating their children. Assuming that the need to be productively engaged in the world is inherent in all humans, in the new vision all that is required of parents is that they provide an environment that is safe, secure, respectful, communicative, encouraging, and disciplined. Whether or not children succeed and measure up is less relevant. What *is* important is that children be allowed the freedom to find some reflection of who they are and what they are becoming as they engage the world. Some children might find themselves engaged in activities that the school systems reward, and other children might pursue less conventional avenues that cannot readily be labeled. But this difference should not be taken to mean that one has failed and the other has measured up. The less-conventional avenues might permit as much self-discovery, self-mastery, and creativity as the activities that the school systematically rewards.

Parents, in providing a productive, secure environment, can trust their own intuitive and experiential skills as adults without worrying that they will fail. It is enough that they are there, present in the environment in which their children are growing. Their children in turn will grow on their own terms, at their own pace, according to their own capacities and strengths. It is enough for parents to accept themselves and their children in their essential humanness. Whether children "achieve" is another matter.

The productive ethic in family life and parenting means creating environments in the home where the productive selves of children and adults are free to emerge and take shape. Opportunities for creative and innovative play, work, building, and producing are foundations for such an environment. A basic trust and respect for human differences and preferences is paramount in creating the environment in the family where all members are free to seek inner commitments and to formulate their own plans for selfhood. As part of a family and parenting agenda for the late 1990s and the new century, it is time to get beyond the Age of the Expert and the preeminence of scientific authority in family life.

Education

Nowhere is the need for a new vision of the productive self more evident than in the educational system. The modern school has nearly supplanted the family as the major socializer of children. No child can escape the influence of the school, and how well children perform their school tasks will be a significant factor in determining their economic futures. Schools have become increasingly important in shaping children's identities, in shaping how they see themselves and their definitions of self-worth. It is in the educational institution that the possibilities of a new vision of the productive self are most crucial, yet I recognize that this very institution could be the most impervious to change. But change it we must if we are to allow our children greater freedom and self-direction in their lives.

There have been many criticisms of contemporary schooling and it is not my intention to review them here. However, the works of authors Samuel Bowles and Herbert Gintis and Ivan Illich are especially relevant.

Bowles and Gintis, in their work *Schooling in Capitalist America*, do much to explode the myth of the meritocratic function of modern education.[9] Their data amply document that the educational system in our society is not based on true meritocratic selection but, rather, exists primarily to legitimize economic inequality. They argue that educational meritocracy is mostly symbolic and that schooling does little to improve the chances for the poor and for racial and ethnic minorities to succeed.

Bowles and Gintis also cite evidence that schools tend to reward docility, passivity, and obedience. Students exhibiting these traits tend to do better in school, to get higher grades, and to win approval from teachers. In fact, traits such as creativity and spontaneity tend to be penalized. Those students who are most approval oriented and measurement conscious are most highly valued and rewarded by teachers. Such an environment encourages school-age children to adopt the measured self as their best chance of success.

No one has leveled more devastating and convincing criticism at modern schooling than Ivan Illich, who argues that schooling fails precisely because it links instruction with certification.[10] Diplomas and degrees become the essential prizes of education. Persons with the most degrees, who have been instructed the longest, are assumed to be the "most educated." Illich contends that nothing could be further from the truth: "In school we are taught that valuable learning is the result of attendance; that the value of learning increases with the amount of input; and, finally that the value can be measured and documented by grades and certificates."[11] Most real learning, however, takes place by "doing and acting" in a setting, Illich argues—not necessarily by institutionalized planning. Lamentably, once societies accept the idea of schooling, all other forms of knowledge and learning are rejected.

Illich also criticizes schools for perpetuating the "myth of measurement of values." Young people are taught that everything can be measured, even their imaginations and their humanity:

> School pretends to break learning up into subject "matters" to build into the pupil a curriculum made of prefabricated blocks and to gauge the result on an international scale. People who submit to the standard of others for the measure of their own personal growth soon apply the same rule to themselves. They no longer have to be put in their place, but put themselves into their assigned slots, squeeze themselves into the niche which they have been taught to seek, and, in the very process, put their fellows into their places too, until everybody and everything fits.[12]

In a schooled society, says Illich, what can't be measured becomes secondary and threatening. Schools thus become the primary arena of measuring-up activities, and education grading systems, test scores, aptitude quotients, and popularity ratings proliferate. Young people are eventually inured to all these processes of measurement. The myth of the measurement of values leads ultimately to the competitive nature of schools, in which school-age children are constantly competing with each other for grades, test scores, and other forms of approval. Children with natural impulses toward creativity, spontaneity, and curiosity soon learn to curb them lest they be labeled a misfit or troublemaker.

Is there the possibility of a new vision in education, a vision that would encourage a more productive ethic in learning and give shape to the productive self in young learners? I think that there is, and it is helpful to turn to the new educational visions being developed by advocates of **cooperative learning,** which emphasizes group learning over individual competition.

To begin with, we need to decide what kind of learning experiences we want young people to have in a complex and changing world. In examining the new models for learning, one theme emerges that challenges the traditional views of education. This theme builds on the idea that a cooperative ethic must replace the competitive ethic in education.

Thomas Lasley and John Bregenzer have set up a model for schooling based on "selflessness."[13] Using a series of propositions, these two educators argue that cooperation in schools is possible and will lead to a more productive learning environment than the traditional competitive model.

For example, Lasley and Bregenzer propose that schools emphasize group welfare over individual welfare. Such an emphasis would move away from ranking systems that hamper a sense of community among students and teachers. Citing the way that simple cultures promote the idea of community problem solving, they argue that this process lessens the pressure on individuals to compete and succeed. Cooperation can be learned and reinforced within the right environment, and schools, using the model of simple cultures, can create such environments. Lasley and Bregenzer suggest that modern school systems suffer from too much hierarchy, that education is inevitably an exercise in authority. By promoting a sense of community in schools, students and staff are able to establish common goals and purposes, breaking down the authority barriers that hamper real learning.

Moreover, Lasley and Bregenzer suggest that involvement replace isolation in schools. One of the educational practices in modern schools that leads to isolation is the use of ability groups based on test scores. Ability groups heighten competition, and students in the lower ability groups experience a sense of isolation, defeat, and loss of self-worth.

The limitations of tracking by ability groups have been documented by Jeannie Oakes and Martin Lipton.[14] According to their studies, tracking does not necessarily lead to achievement for average and low-ability students. Moreover, high-ability students have been shown to progress just as well in mixed-ability classes. Oakes and Lipton argue that tracking by ability groups does not promote greater levels of self-esteem among the low-ability students.

The tracking model dates to the nineteenth-century model of schooling, reflecting the industrial culture of U.S. society. In this model, school curricula revolve around the technology of testing, a factory model of efficiency, and the use of grades for student evaluation. Oakes and Lipton contend that educators took for granted that there were basic differences in children that could be measured. Thus, these differences were structured into the curricula.[15] Today, as we have seen, the idea of measured differences among students is one that dies hard.

Competition in education produces isolation and reduces a sense of mutuality among students. Without a sense of shared responsibility, students become ego-centered, and those students who perform well learn to lack any compassion toward those students who don't measure up.

Finally, Lasley and Bregenzer contend that one of the most important lessons students can learn in schools is a sense of responsibility. Students must learn to be accountable for their actions. Students have not only a responsibility to themselves but also a responsibility to their fellow students and to their community. Interestingly, these authors suggest that one of the most effective ways to promote a feeling of responsibility among students is to give them experiences in caring for and nurturing others. They argue that the modern household has virtually eliminated chores; young people don't carry out productive work around the house to help the family survive. Children are robbed of their opportunity to contribute to the welfare of their most immediate communities. Schools can create the feeling of community responsibility in students by allowing them to perform nurturing activities with and for others. As an illustration, several alternative schools in the United States require students to do volunteer work in the community, working in nursing homes, day care centers, and so on.[16] All of this can be viewed as part of productive learning.

Grade competition produces a hostile learning environment in which too many students feel isolated and unimportant. Competing for grades leads to overconformity and encourages an approval-oriented and self-centered selfhood. Cooperative models in education, on the other hand, reward and encourage group problem solving and group processes. When group problem solving is encouraged, the sense of community is strengthened. Under less pressure for individual grades, students don't feel so anxious about having to measure up continually. When group efforts are emphasized, students learn to accept responsibility for their behavior and develop more compassionate responses to their fellow students. As students become more comfortable in a less competitive environment, they might well have less need to form the rigid, conformist types of peer groups that now characterize the school setting. Though peer groups will still flourish in a productive and cooperative learning environment, the peer group could extend and encourage better relations among students.

Learning in cooperative groups can also contribute to educational achievement when both individual as well as group accountability are required. Robert E. Slavin, who has studied the effects of cooperative learning for years, tells us: "Research on cooperative learning has established that these methods can be very effective in increasing student achievement in many subjects and grade levels when student groups are rewarded on the basis of the average learning of the group members."[17]

This cooperative-group approach in education is really more consistent with the newer styles of management being employed in industry and work in the United States. Allowing students greater opportunities for group problem solving in the schools gives them important presocialization into organizational and work environments.

School Inequality

The issue of equality in the public schools has been the topic of many books and much debate. Any number of solutions have been proposed and tried, from court-ordered busing to voucher systems to calls for greater school accountability. Inequities in school funding is indeed one problem, amply documented and denounced by many critics. Jonathon Kozol is one among several who have written convincing accounts of the deplorable conditions found in many inner-city schools, where real learning is severely hampered.[18]

A new vision for addressing the issue of unequal funding of schools must include a reform of the tax structure and of the mechanisms by which public education is paid for. It is obvious that many students in poor school districts do not receive the quality of education that students receive in affluent communities. How can these students be expected to compete in the technically sophisticated career market that will characterize our future economy? It is beyond the scope of this book to provide a detailed plan for school refinancing. But one modest proposal that is being tried in some states is to finance public schools through state funds rather than through local property taxes. State monies, gathered through sales and income taxes, can be more equitably distributed to public schools. The local-property-tax model for school funding will inevitably lead to the systematic inequalities that put racial and class minorities at such a disadvantage in today's economy. Surely the time is right for innovative plans to create greater equity in funding our public schools.

Gender equity issues have plagued our educational system as well. We have seen in earlier chapters that gender stereotyping creates problems for both men and women. However, the issue goes beyond concerns with body imagery, self-esteem, and personal attractiveness. **Gender-biased education,** in which gender stereotypes are subtly or overtly imposed on students, has led to problems for women in achieving their full academic potentials.

Research has identified the ways that gender bias occurs in the educational system. Textbooks, educational materials, testing, and school activities have all been gender biased in ways that favor male accomplishment and put women at a disadvantage. Pamela Keating, writing about sex equity in schools, presents evidence that women are subtly discouraged from courses in math and science as well as related careers because of gender bias in academic and career counseling.[19] Many school counselors see math and science as male domains with respect to both academic achievement and career potential. In texts and school curricula, the experiences of women are often slighted or ignored completely. Moreover, female students are often rewarded by teachers for being passive, quiet, and approval oriented. Such rewarded traits can cause women students to hide their academic deficiencies and weaknesses, thus preventing them from getting the help they need to succeed.

Keating offers us two solutions for achieving greater gender equity in our schools that will enhance opportunities for women in education. First, she believes that teacher preparation programs should be reformed. Future teachers must learn how to develop a greater range of student abilities and how to respond to a wider variety of student capacities. All students must be taught to find meaning in life, and future teachers must learn to develop their students' critical reasoning abilities. Teacher preparation programs must instill in teachers a toleration for all kinds of student diversity, including, crucially, gender. Second, Keating suggests that since gender is socially constructed, education can be an important vehicle for creating sex-equitable opportunity. School activities, curricula, testing, materials, and even organization must be structured to eliminate gender bias and to promote gender equity. Students should be able to use their educational experiences to get beyond gender stereotypes and acquire a greater sensitivity to the rights of both genders to acquire knowledge and to move to their full academic and career potential.

University Life

Since most readers of this book are college students, perhaps it is necessary to include some suggestions for making college academic life less pressured and more meaningful. Earlier we noted that many college students were subjected to the pressures of maintaining high GPAs and doing well on standardized tests for admission to graduate schools. The college experience was no respite from measurement mania. Two developments are worth noting that may lessen some of the academic pressure for college students. How effective they will be remains to be seen, but they are steps in the right direction.

Some graduate programs are now beginning to value alternative means of assessing academic potential for students. Though standardized tests are not being abandoned, graduate school admissions committees are now considered student experiences, written work, and motivation as important elements in assessment. For example, at the University of North Texas, prospective doctoral students with masters degrees and low GRE scores are allowed to apply for conditional admission into the sociology program. These students are allowed to submit undergraduate papers, theses, and other written work or publications as part of their application. Often these materials will tell the department admissions committee more about the student's potential than scores on a GRE or even GPAs.

An even more appealing mechanism for relieving academic pressure for college students is a "time off" from college. Colin Hall and Ron Lieber have described this phenomenon in their book *Taking Time Off*.[20] They describe the experiences of a variety of college students who interrupted their college careers to work full time, to travel, or to volunteer. Often this hiatus provided students with greater motivation, maturity, and career focus upon their return to college. Moreover, some students found that employers were not put off by this break in career preparation. Often employers are looking for some experience anyway from students, and what better way to gain work experience than taking time off from college? Maturity helps a student adapt to the academic pressures generated by college life. A time-off period can increase maturity and personal growth, making a student much more academically capable when he or she does return to campus.

Though time off is not for all college students, those who have tried it have found that the benefits seem greater than the liabilities. For students really feeling the pressures of measured academic success, a time off, even for a semester, might produce a whole new focus on academic life.

The Economy and Work

Under the present vision, the measured self is the result of an economic and work system that reveres only measurable results (income, promotion, and so on), that promotes excessive competition and power struggles between genders, and that contributes to demeaning gender stereotyping. Men and women, instead of finding their life's significance in creative and meaningful work, are often trapped in a dehumanizing struggle to obtain the commercial and material trappings of success. And standards of success are externally imposed and constantly shifting due to the ebb and flow of events on Wall Street and Madison Avenue. Rather than being free to choose the most productive and creative avenues to fulfillment, adults pursue the most socially approved lines of gender and status conformity.

Moreover, the performance ethic in the present vision leads to excessive reliance on credentials in allocating rewards and privileges. Credentialing is used to ensure the privilege of some groups and to keep other groups in relatively permanent positions of poverty and unemployment. U.S. society can be characterized as a system of winners and losers, with the losers slipping farther behind in the credential race, their realistic chances of finding any kind of success and dignified work in the present economy increasingly slim.

Is it possible that in the decades to come we can create an economic structure that will allow people to lead more productive and meaningful work lives and at the same time distribute economic and social justice more equally? Or are these goals somehow incompatible? I argue that a productive self can emerge in economy and work and that, at the same time, we can create greater opportunities for the poor and minorities to enjoy the fruits of a productive life as well.

Currently, there are two views about the feasibility of using public policy to even out the playing field in the economic reward structure of society.

One model argues that public policy is essentially fruitless in helping poor minorities since the problem lies not in economic injustice but with the poor themselves. The poor are considered deficient in intelligence and that deficit is held to account for their continued low placement in the class structure. This view is represented in the famous **bell curve argument** of Charles Murray and Richard J. Herrnstein, which is that early intervention programs for the poor are ineffective since the poor lack basic intelligence.[21]

The bell curve argument has been rightly and justly critiqued by a number of sociologists, including William J. Wilson, who holds the alternative view that supports public policy in economic reform. Wilson's recent study of the new urban poor, *When Work Disappears,* contains effective criticism of Murray and Herrnstein's position.[22] Wilson cogently demonstrates that the intelligence tests used by Herrnstein and Murray measure not genetic endowment but cultural achievement. Moreover, the bell curve argument does not sufficiently account for what Wilson calls the "accumulation of negative environmental differences." In other words, the economic life chances of a group are very much shaped by the sorts of environmental stimuli, opportunities, and values that the group is exposed to. Wilson's argument is not only compelling but is realistic and pragmatic in its insistence on viable public policy to assist the losers in the U.S. economy. This final section will summarize Wilson's findings concerning the new urban poor.

Wilson contends that poverty in urban ghettos is nothing new. However, the older ghettos had more working poor, which meant that work values, networks, and access avenues were still in place. Poverty in the contemporary ghetto is more likely to be jobless poverty, and, when high levels of joblessness persist, work values and occupational networking tend to decline.

Wilson finds that work has all but vanished in many inner-city neighborhoods, due in some measure to the decline in the economic opportunities for low-skilled workers. The new global economy has lead to a steady decline in manufacturing jobs in U.S. cities, and jobs are tending to move out of cities into suburban areas.[23] Overall, there has been a general decline in mass production in the United States. The inner-city poor are especially vulnerable to the job loss associated with this decline. Wilson finds that the poverty rate in Chicago's Black Belt increased 20 percent from 1970 to 1990.

The emerging economic opportunities in the United States are in the skilled and technological fields that require sophisticated and lengthy educations. Wilson finds that today nearly all improvements in productivity are due to technology and human capital (superior education.) The current economy needs highly skilled, sophisticated, and well-educated workers, that is, workers with the sorts of credentials in short supply among inner-city adults. Less-skilled jobs are vanishing and are poorly paid.

In the global, highly competitive economy, corporations can either improve productivity or lower wages to remain competitive. Too many U.S. companies have chosen the latter alternative. Interestingly, businessman Richard C. Haas argued in 1996 that it is a misconception for companies to think that retrenchment and trimming employment rosters will raise workers' productivity.[24] He argues that productivity is really the capacity of men and women to add value to goods and services in excess of costs. This capacity—to add value to the economy—is uniquely human. In Haas's view, the challenge for companies is to find new markets that require the hiring of more humans as "value adders." This is a more productive alternative to downsizing.

Without this sort of change in emphasis, the ill effects of the global economy that Wilson documents will continue. In Wilson's view, international capital is now so mobile that there is no guarantee that economic growth will help those in one's own backyard. For example, in the United States, unemployment has been kept down by getting workers to accept more low-wage jobs.

Wilson's vision of the economic change necessary to redress the problems of the urban poor include reinvigorating public policy. Unfortunately, as Wilson himself recognizes, our society has systematically retreated from public policy in recent decades. The current political buzzwords are "less government," "privatization," and "personal responsibility."

Undaunted, Wilson argues that the social rights of people are as important as their political and civil rights.[25] He contends that compared to other industrialized nations, we do far less to cushion working families from the downside of the global economy. His suggested reforms include greater accountability of public schools; more federal support of public schools, especially in areas where tax bases are low; family policies that support the lives of children; and more job opportunities for high school only graduates. With respect to this last reform, Wilson maintains that too often our present educational emphasis is limited to getting students into college. For non–college bound students, there is little transition from high school into work. Consequently, older teens and young adults have few decent job possibilities and thus little chance to advance on the job. Wilson cites one study showing that only 42 percent of those black youths not enrolled in college held jobs the October after graduating high school in June. This is compared to 69 percent of white youth.[26]

Finally, Wilson argues for a Work Projects Administration (WPA)–style jobs program to put inner-city youth to work on urban infrastructure. Jobs and training should be required and provided for all young adults and not just those on welfare. Though the government should be the employer of last resort, in the short run, Wilson argues, it makes more sense for young adults to work and job-network than to remain idle. There is much infrastructure work to be done in U.S. cities, and there are many needing work and training.

The anti–public policy forces are strong and determined, and they appear to have public opinion on their side. On the other hand, the United States has had a tradition of effective public policy to address the issues of poverty, housing, and job training. We all know there is much productive work to be done. Where private firms find it unprofitable, public institutions must find it necessary and vital and begin securing jobs for people who need them.

As the United States is poised to face an even more competitive global economy in the next century, can we really afford a retreat from public policy that addresses the needs of those least prepared to measure up? Doesn't government have some role to play in balancing the scales of economic justice and fairness? Isn't it time to reaffirm our commitment to values of equity and fairness in our economic life, especially where public policy is concerned?

The new vision of the productive self offers fresh possibilities of being, relatedness, and productivity for Americans if we choose to reorient our values and self-definitions. We have the promise of opportunities to redirect American culture and selfhood, to live more productively, cooperatively, and meaningfully. We may well usher in a period when adults and children are less pressured to measure up to countless standards of competence, perfection, success, and beauty and more free to enter into productive and creative relations with others as they seek to build and live in a world more in their own image and to their own liking.

Key Terms

1. The New Vision
2. The Productive Self

3.   Cooperative Learning
4.   Gender-Biased Education
5.   The Bell Curve Argument

Review Questions

1. What characterizes selfhood in the present vision?
2. What is meant by the productive self?
3. What advice to parents seems most consistent with the productive self?
4. Describe some of the criticisms of schooling in its present form.
5. What are the advantages of cooperative learning in education?
6. Describe some of the ways education can be gender biased. How can gender bias be reduced?
7. State the advantages that a "time off" from college study might have for college students.
8. What does Wilson think is the significance of widespread joblessness in U.S. inner cities?
9. Describe the reforms that Wilson suggests to alleviate inner-city poverty.

Discussion Questions

1. Discuss how some people can be comfortable in the measured self.
2. Do you think it is possible today to encourage parents to be less concerned with raising "successful children"?
3. What sorts of parenting skills do you feel will contribute to the productive self? Do you agree with those suggested by the author?
4. Reflect on your school career; did you have opportunities for cooperative learning? If so, how did you respond to this type of learning?
5. What do you think of taking a "time off" from college? Can it relieve academic pressure on college students? Have you taken a "time off," or would you be willing to take one?
6. Suggest some of your own ideas to reduce gender bias in schools and education.
7. Why do you think that there has been such a retreat from public policy in solving issues related to the economy and urban life?
8. Discuss Wilson's agenda for dealing with black urban poverty. What do you think of his suggestions for WPA-style employment to put the urban poor back to work?

9. Of the changes in family life, education, and economy/work formulated by the author, which ones are most likely to lead to a more productive self?

Activities

1. Conduct a small literature search on cooperative learning and its impact on education. You might try to find some information on how cooperative learning can improve instruction in mathematics and science since these subjects are often difficult for many students. Present your findings to the class and discuss the implications of cooperative learning in education today. (You might use the ERIC database search using key words mathematics, gender, and cooperative learning.)
2. If your college or university has a women's studies department or curriculum, interview the director. Inquire about his or her views of gender equity on the campus. How satisfied is he or she with the university's policies with regard to gender equity? What changes would he or she suggest to improve the quality of life for women on the campus? Report your findings back to the class.

Notes

Chapter 1

1. James Vander Zanden, *Sociology: The Core* (New York: Knopf, 1986), p. 125.
2. George Ritzer, *The McDonaldization of Society* (Thousand Oaks, Calif.: Pine Forge Press, 1994).
3. C. Wright Mills, *The Sociological Imagination* (New York: Oxford University Press, 1959).

Chapter 2

1. Charles Horton Cooley, *Human Nature and Social Order* (New York: Scribner, 1902).
2. George Herbert Mead, *Mind, Self, and Society* (Chicago: University of Chicago Press, 1934), p. 154.
3. Sheldon B. Korones, *High Risk Newborn Infants* (St. Louis), Mo.: C. V. Mosby, 1981).
4. Philip Aries, *Centuries of Childhood* (New York: Knopf, 1981).
5. Ibid., p. 411.
6. David Elkind, *The Hurried Child* (Reading, Mass.: Addison-Wesley, 1981).
7. Howard James, *Children in Trouble* (New York: David McKay, 1969).
8. Letty Pogrebin, "The Secret Fear That Keeps Us from Raising Free Children," in Laurel Richardson and Verta Taylor, eds., *Feminist Frontiers: Rethinking Sex, Gender, and Society* (Reading, Mass.: Addison-Wesley, 1983).
9. Barbara Ehrenreich, *The Hearts of Men* (Garden City, N.Y.: Anchor Press/Doubleday, 1983).
10. David Elkind, *The Ties That Stress: The New Family Imbalance* (Cambridge, Mass.: Harvard University Press, 1994).
11. Barbara Ehrenreich and Dierdre English, *For Her Own Good* (Garden City, N.Y.: Anchor Press/Doubleday, 1979).
12. Christopher Lasch, *Haven in a Heartless World* (New York: Basic Books, 1979).
13. Sheila Kitzinger, *Women and Mothers* (New York: Vintage Books, 1978).

14. Karen Levine, "Overstressed Kids," *Parents Magazine*, December 1993, p. 246.

15. David Elkind, *Ties That Stress.*

16. John Seely, Alexander Sim, and Elizabeth Loosley, *Crestwood Heights* (New York: John Wiley, 1963).

17. Daniel Goleman, *Emotional Intelligence* (New York: Bantam Books, 1995).

Chapter 3

1. Alex Thio, *Sociology* (New York: HarperCollins, 1996).

2. Erving Goffman, *The Presentation of Self in Everyday Life* (Garden City, N.Y.: Doubleday, 1959).

3. Charles E. Basch and Theresa B. Kersch, "Adolescent Perceptions of Stressful Life Events," *Health Education*, June/July 1986, p. 4.

4. Thio, op. cit., pp. 156–157.

5. George H. Mead, *Mind, Self, and Other* (Chicago: University of Chicago Press, 1934).

6. Jan Krukowski, "What Do Students Want? Status," *Change*, May/June 1985, pp. 21–28.

7. David Elkind, "Stress and the Middle-Grader," *The School Counselor* 33 (January 1986):196–206.

8. David Owen, *None of the Above: Behind the Myth of Scholastic Aptitude* (Boston: Houghton-Mifflin, 1985).

9. Daniel Goleman, *Emotional Intelligence* (New York: Bantam Books, 1995).

10. A. P. Schoff, "Drug Problems in Athletics—It's Not Only the Pros," *U.S. News and World Report*, October 17, 1983, pp. 164–166.

11. D. M. Garner et al., "Cultural Expectations of Thinness in Women," *Psychological Reports* 47 (1980):483–491.

12. Susie Orbach, *Hunger Strike: The Anorectic's Struggle as a Metaphor for Our Age* (New York: Norton, 1986).

13. Marlene Boskind-Lodahl, "Cinderella's Step-Sisters: A Feminist Perspective on Anorexia Nervosa and Bulimia," *Signs: A Journal of Women in Culture and Society* 2 (1976):342–356.

14. Karen S. Schneider, "Mission Impossible," *People*, June 3, 1996, pp. 64–74.

15. Philip Slater, *The Pursuit of Loneliness* (Boston: Beacon Press, 1970).

16. Craig B. Little, *Deviance and Control* (Itasca, Minn.: F. E. Peacock, 1995).

17. Cited in James W. Coleman and Donald R. Cressey, *Social Problems* (New York: HarperCollins, 1996), p. 275.

18. Emile Durkheim, *Suicide* (New York: The Free Press, 1966).

19. "The Copycat Suicider," *Newsweek*, March 23, 1987, pp. 28–29.

20. Elizabeth Gleick, "Playing the Numbers," *Time*, April 17, 1995, p. 52.

21. Quoted in Krukowski, op. cit.

22. David L. Warren, "Pizza, Popcorn, and the President," *Change*, May/June 1985, p. 29.

23. David Elkind, *All Grown Up and No Place to Go* (Reading, Mass.: Addison-Wesley, 1984).

Chapter 4

1. David A. Ward and Lorene H. Stone, *Sociology* (St. Paul: West Publishing, 1996).

2. Alex Thio, *Sociology* (New York: HarperCollins, 1996).

3. *New York Magazine*, January 20, 1986.

4. *Mother Earth News*, March/April 1986.

5. David Reisman, *The Lonely Crowd* (New Haven: Yale University Press, 1950).

6. Joe L. Dubbert, "Progressivism and the Masculinity Crisis," in Elizabeth Pleck and Joseph Pleck, eds., *The American Man* (Englewood Cliffs, N.J.: Prentice-Hall, 1980).

7. Peter Stearns, *Be a Man: Males in Modern Society* (New York: Holmes and Meier, 1979).

8. Ward and Stone, op. cit., p. 363.

9. Shoshona Zuboff, "New Worlds of Computers-Mediated Work," in Hugh Lena, William Helmreich, and William McCord, eds., *Contemporary Issues in Society* (New York: McGraw-Hill, 1992).

10. Andrew Kimbrell, *The Masculine Mystique: The Politics of Masculinity* (New York: Ballantine, 1995).

11. Marc Fasteau, *The Male Machine* (New York: McGraw-Hill, 1974), p. 33.

12. Kimbrell, op. cit.

13. Steven Florio, quoted in *Common Cause Magazine*, March/April 1985, p. 8.

14. Nancy Chodorow, *The Reproduction of Mothering* (Berkeley: University of California Press, 1978).

15. "Cross-Addiction: Surprising Results of the Ms. Survey," *Ms. Magazine*, February 1987, pp. 44–47.

16. Pete Hamill, "Great Expectations," *Ms.*, September 1986, pp. 34–83.

17. Carol Osborn, *Enough Is Enough: Exploding the Myth of Having It All* (New York: F. P. Putnams, 1986).

18. Hamill, op. cit., p. 37.

19. James W. Coleman and Donald R. Cressey, *Social Problems* (New York: HarperCollins, 1996).

20. Ibid., p. 303.

21. Ibid., p. 305.

22. "The New Calvinists: Are They Climbing the Ladder to Nowhere?" *The Indianapolis Star*, November 25, 1986, p. 16.

23. Ibid.

24. Ibid.

25. "Fear and Loathing at High School Reunions," *Psychology Today*, 25 (March/April 1992), pp. 68–71.

26. Ibid., p. 69.

27. Ibid., p. 70.

28. Ibid., pp. 69–70.

29. Joan Liebman-Smith, "Sex: The Tyranny of Frequency, or When Enough Is Enough," *Ms.*, April 1987, pp. 78–89.

30. Kimbrell, op. cit.

Chapter 5

1. David Newman, *Sociology* (Thousand Oaks, Calif.: Pine Forge Press, 1995).

2. Jerry Adler, "The Overclass: How the New Elite Scrambled Up the Merit Ladder—and Wants to Stay There Any Way It Can," *Newsweek*, July 31, 1995, pp. 35–46.

3. Newman, op. cit., p. 341.

4. Donald L. Barlett and James B. Steele, "America: Who Stole the Dream?" reported in *The Indianapolis Star*, September 22, 1996, A8.

5. Cited in Mary H. Cooper, "Reality of American Dream Is Fading," *The Indianapolis Star*, November 11, 1995, A9.

6. Robert H. Frank and Philip J. Cook, *The Winner-Take-All Society* (New York: Free Press, 1995).

7. Barlett and Steele, op. cit., September 25, 1996, A1.

8. Ibid., September 24, 1996, C2.

9. N. R. Kleinfield, "The Company as One Big Happy Family, No More," *New York Times*, March 4, 1996, A1–A14.

10. Ibid., p. A12.

11. Barlett and Steele, op. cit., September 25, 1996, A8.

12. Elliot Currie and Jerome Skolnick, *America's Problems: Social Issues and Public Policy* (Boston: Little, Brown and Co., 1984).

13. Joe R. Feagin, *Social Problems: A Critical Power Conflict Perspective* (Englewood Cliffs, N.J.: Prentice-Hall, 1986).

14. Harry Braverman, *Labor and Monopoly Capital* (New York: Monthly Review Press, 1975).

15. Ivar Berg, *Education and Jobs: The Great Training Robbery* (New York: Praeger Publishers, 1970).

16. Barbara Ehrenreich, *The Hearts of Men* (New York: Doubleday, 1983).

17. Ruth Sidel, *Women and Children Last* (New York: Viking Penguin, 1987).

18. Katherine S. Newman, *Falling from Grace* (New York: Vintage Books, 1988).

19. Sidel, op. cit.

20. Newman, op. cit., p. 342.

21. David A. Ward and Lorene H. Stone, *Sociology* (St. Paul: West Publishing, 1996), p. 237.

22. Newman, op. cit., p. 427.

23. Barlett and Steele, op. cit., September 25, 1996, A1.

24. Ibid.

25. Ibid., September 25, 1996, A8.

26. Ward and Stone, op. cit., p. 214.

27. Stan Warren, "A Generation of Talent America Can't Afford to Lose," *Cleveland Plain Dealer*, October 22, 1987, p. 11C.

28. Ward and Stone, op. cit., p. 215.

29. Ibid., p. 218.

30. Ibid., p. 219.

31. Steven A. Holmes, "For Hispanic Poor, No Silver Lining," *New York Times*, October 13, 1996, Sec. 3, p. 5.

32. Ward and Stone, op. cit., p. 219.

33. Ibid., p. 220.

34. Randall Collins, *The Credential Spiral* (New York: Academic Press, 1979).

35. Kathy Hogan Trocheck, "Preschool Panic," *The Atlanta Constitution*, April 9, 1987, pp. 1–4B.

36. Jill Smolowe, "Bake Sales," *Time*, April 24, 1995.

37. William Ryan, *Blaming the Victim* (New York: Random House, 1972).

38. Lillian B. Rubin, *Families on the Fault Line* (New York: HarperCollins, 1994).

Chapter 6

1. C. Wright Mills, *The Sociological Imagination* (New York: Oxford University Press, 1959).

2. Ibid.

3. David Newman, *Sociology* (Thousand Oaks, Calif.: Pine Forge Press, 1995), p. 18.

4. Erich Fromm, *The Sane Society* (New York: Reinhart, 1955).

5. Erich Fromm, *Escape from Freedom* (New York: Avon, 1965).

6. Erich Fromm, *Sane Society*.

7. Christopher Lasch, *Haven in a Heartless World* (New York: Basic Books, 1977).

8. Ibid., p. 172.

9. Samuel Bowles and Herbert Gintis, *Schooling in Capitalist America* (New York: Basic Books, 1976).

10. Ivan Illich, *Deschooling Society* (New York: Harper and Row, 1970).

11. Ibid., p. 39.

12. Ibid., p. 40.

13. Thomas Lasley and John Bregenzer, "Toward Selflessness," *Journal of Human Behavior and Learning* 33 (1986): pp. 20–27.

14. Jeannie Oakes and Martin Lipton, "Tracking and Ability Grouping: A Structural Barrier to Access and Achievement," in John I. Goodlad and Pamela Keating, eds., *Access to Knowledge* (New York: College Board Publications, 1994), pp. 187–204.

15. Ibid.

16. Ruth Steele, "Jefferson County Open High School—Philosophy and Purpose," *Holistic Education* 1, no. 2 (1988): pp. 35–38.

17. Robert E. Slavin, *Educational Psychology: Theory into Practice* (Needham Heights, Mass.: Allyn and Bacon, 1991), p. 355.

18. Jonathon Kozol, *Savage Inequalities* (New York: Harper and Row, 1991).

19. Pamela Keating, "Striving for Sex Equity in Schools," in John I. Goodlad and Pamela Keating, eds., *Access to Knowledge* (New York: College Board Publications, 1994), pp. 91–106.

20. Colin Hall and Ron Lieber, *Taking Time Off* (New York: Noonday Press, 1996).

21. Richard J. Herrnstein and Charles Murray, *The Bell Curve: Intelligence and Class in American Life* (New York: Free Press, 1994).

22. William J. Wilson, *When Work Disappears* (New York: Knopf, 1996).

23. Ibid., p. 28.

24. Richard C. Haas, "A Catholic Alternative to Downsizing," *America*, June 8, 1996, pp. 18–20.

25. Wilson, op. cit., p. 161.

26. Ibid., p. 217.

About the Book and Author

Measuring Up explores the relentless pressure that many Americans feel to measure up successfully with respect to grades, beauty, economic achievement, and various quantified "aptitudes." This unique text focuses on both the macro and micro aspects of social and cultural life, discussing such topics as culture, socialization, peer groups, reference groups, presentations of self, gender roles, class inequality, deindustrialization, corporate downsizing, status systems, and human agency. The author takes a critical look at the modern cultural values that support the performance ethic and concludes with hope for a reorientation of cultural values that could promote a more productive, authentic selfhood in the United States.

James M. Mannon is professor of sociology at DePauw University and the author of *American Gridmark*.

Index